I've met some fine scientists who are decent theol[...] theologians who are as comfortable with the wor[...] you think Van Sloten's approach is to simply see [...] world, then you've seriously underestimated the [...] Van Sloten looks much deeper and finds nothing [...] center of scientific inquiry, from ecosystems to a[...] This work challenges the scientist to experience God's manifest p[...] science and opens the eyes of the theologian to be able to read God's "other" book—the natural world and its holy complexity.

GREGORY A. KLINE, MD, Clinical Professor of Medicine/Endocrinology, University of Calgary

Can it be? Are there pathways to knowing God through science? In his new book, *God Speaks Science*, John Van Sloten guides us down a seldom trod path of knowing God through contemplative examination of scientific discoveries and the roads leading to them. This book is imaginative and revelatory; it contains a well-written series of interesting vignettes while illuminating a neglected area of spiritual inquiry.

GEORGE CHACONAS, Professor Cumming School of Medicine, University of Calgary

I'm not a scientist, but I have always loved trees and stars and music. Even as a boy I perked up when we sang "all nature sings and 'round me rings the music of the spheres" or "thou rising morn in praise rejoice, ye lights of evening, find a voice," because even with the most basic knowledge of Jesus I sensed Him speaking—singing, even—through His creation. I still do. The church has a long and beautiful tradition of learning what God is like, not just by reading Scripture, but also by delighting in and studying His creation—and with this book John Van Sloten has done both.

ANDREW PETERSON, singer-songwriter; author of *The God of the Garden* and The Wingfeather Saga

Questions about the relationship between science and Christian faith are numerous and often difficult. Pastor John Van Sloten has given us wonderful answers to many of these questions in this outstanding and deeply religious book. He beautifully illustrates the harmony between science and Christianity by focusing on several specific fields of science, from medicine and molecular biology to astrophysics, geology, and linguistics. The profound insights the author shares with us are too many to count but can be summarized as pure doxology. Van Sloten uses the human study of God's creation to extract awareness of its fundamental beauty and majesty of the Creator. This book is for everyone, scientist or not, Bible scholar or not, even Christian or not. God does indeed speak science, and this book tells us how.

SY GARTE, professor at New York University, Rutgers University, and the University of Pittsburgh; Director at the NIH; former member of the Templeton Foundation's board of directors

Theologians have long described Scripture and nature as two books of God's revelation; now Pastor John Van Sloten digs deep into this truth. He actively reads the two books together, with "the Bible shining light on creation and creation bringing deeper understanding to the Scriptures." John introduces fascinating examples from many fields of science and medicine and draws thought-provoking parallels to theological truths. He invites us to engage with more than our reason—to ponder God's creation in our hearts and turn in worship to the Author of it all.

DEB HAARSMA, astrophysicist and President of BioLogos

As the father of four intellectually curious children and the pastor of a church filled with college students, professors, and PhD candidates, I was thrilled by every page of this masterful and beautiful exploration of the way God reveals Himself through the created world. John Van Sloten provides us with a long overdue reminder that God is in constant communication with us through the physical world if we will pause long enough to listen, look, taste, feel, and smell His beautiful handiwork. The skies declare His glory, the earth rejoices, the sea resounds, the fields are jubilant, and the trees of the forest sing for joy. Every atom in the universe reverberates with the surpassing genius of God's divine intent. Van Sloten's book reminds us that if God made the world, then science is a form of worship that leads us beyond knowledge and into awe and wonder. Dive in and enjoy!
BRENT ROAM, Lead Pastor, One Family Church

John Van Sloten has the innate ability to take complicated issues and make them easy to understand. His writing seamlessly intertwines the mysteries of faith with the realities of science, which leads to an engaging read no matter where your belief system sits.
MONICA ZUROWSKI, Calgary Herald deputy editor, journalist, and Canadian bestselling author

God Speaks Science is a book of delight, awe, and joy. It's about science and God but not in any of the ways you might expect. If you're wanting to read about the *two books* of God (creation and revelation) in a way that draws you into a fresh sense of love toward the One who made all things and is making all things new—read this book. Through nontechnical storytelling, experience the world of science and nature in fresh, amazing ways. Who would have imagined seeing God through the wonder of our knees? John invites you into some ways science illuminates one of God's two books and then invites you to dwell and meditate on these stories.
ALAN ROXBURGH, teacher, missiologist, and author of 15 books, including *Joining God in the Great Unraveling: Where Are We and What Have I Learned*

Too often, conversations surrounding science and religion are either simplistic or a rehash of old and tired debates. But Rev. John Van Sloten approaches the interaction of these two worlds with great humility and deep respect for the nature of science—and, even more importantly, the scientists themselves. This book will inspire you to see the unseen spirituality of radiation, the sacredness of water, and the transcendence of deep-sea creatures. Most of all, it will make you rethink the way science and religion can come together to enhance a sense of awe and majesty surrounding the natural world.
RABBI GEOFFREY A. MITELMAN, Founding Director, Sinai and Synapses

In *God Speaks Science*, pastor and writer John Van Sloten has taken on a noble task—closing the Christian's imagined gap between faith in God and a critical trust in science. As only a loving pastor could, the author teaches with one eye on the truth and the other on the fact that untangling misunderstandings and untruths in the human heart is rarely a one-and-done affair. With patience and scholarship, Van Sloten breaks down a complicated, centuries-old problem. He serves up to his readers a fresh retelling of the beautiful compatibility between knowing God and the vocation of knowing God's creativity. All human enterprise has its failures, including science. In fact, the scientific method accounts for this. Hopefully, because of this well-written book, more Christians will find delight in unpacking the micro and the macro of creation. There's no threat. Discovery and thanksgiving await the curious.
CHARLIE PEACOCK, Grammy award-winning music producer, author, and Founder/Director Emeritus of the Commercial Music Program, Lipscomb University

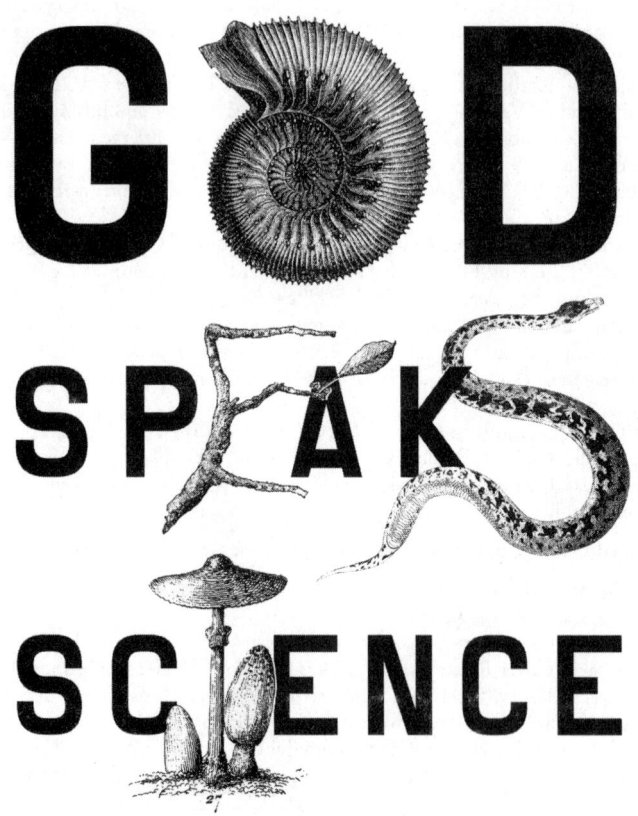

GOD SPEAKS SCIENCE

WHAT NEURONS, GIANT SQUID, AND
SUPERNOVAE REVEAL ABOUT OUR CREATOR

JOHN VAN SLOTEN

MOODY PUBLISHERS

CHICAGO

To my wife, Fran—a non-scientist
whose deep faith enabled her to engage God
through so many science-based sermons and book chapters.

CONTENTS

ENGAGING GOD
THROUGH ALL THINGS

In the beginning was the Word,
and the Word was with God,
and the Word was God.
He was with God in the beginning.
Through him all things *were made.*

JOHN 1:1-3, *emphasis mine*

I've never been much of an empirical thinker. While I was growing up, the languages of physics, chemistry, and biology didn't come naturally to me. Like many non-scientist types I completed the requisite high school science courses with average marks and bid the topic farewell. Apart from a tangential brush with physics in an undergraduate structural engineering course, I got along without science just fine.

But then things changed. After a dramatic spiritual awakening I decided to switch careers, study theology, and become a preacher. At first, my lack of scientific proficiency wasn't a problem—my text, after all, was the Bible, and my tools were ancient languages, systematic theology, and church history. But, a few years into my new calling,

I woke up to a very old truth (the seeds of which had been hiding in my church denomination's theological tradition for centuries). It was the idea that God *speaks* through the creation:

> In the beginning God created the heavens and the earth.
> **GEN. 1:1**

> The heavens declare the glory of God;
>   the skies proclaim the work of his hands.
> Day after day they pour forth speech;
>   night after night they reveal knowledge.
> They have no speech, they use no words;
>   no sound is heard from them.
> Yet their voice goes out into all the earth,
>   their words to the ends of the world. **PS. 19:1-4**

> For since the creation of the world God's invisible qualities—his eternal power and divine nature—have been clearly seen, being understood from what has been made. **ROM. 1:20**

According to the apostle Paul, God can be clearly seen through what has been made. The universe reveals God's invisible qualities. God spoke through creation long before speaking through the Bible.

This is what Christians throughout history have believed about divine revelation—that God speaks through *two books*—the Bible and creation. Each is a means through which God can be known and experienced. Both Scripture and God's creation are authoritative texts.

When I was a teenager, I had to memorize a portion of the sixteenth-century *Belgic Confession* (addressing "The Means by Which We Know God") for a catechism class:

We know God by two means:

First, by the creation, preservation, and government of the universe, since that universe is before our eyes like a beautiful book in which all creatures, great and small, are as letters to make us ponder the invisible things of God: God's eternal power and divinity, as the apostle Paul says in Romans 1:20.

All these things are enough to convict humans and to leave them without excuse.

Second, God makes himself known to us more clearly by his holy and divine Word, as much as we need in this life, for God's glory and for our salvation.[1]

For a person of faith, these two books connect synergistically. When we know God (more clearly) through the written Word, we can know God (more clearly) through creational Words. The Bible, John Calvin taught, sharpens our vision like a pair of glasses.[2] When viewed through the lens of the Scriptures, creation becomes a theater of God's glory.[3] While the nature of this theater is equally accessible to all humanity (regardless of their faith or non-faith traditions) and the experience of God's glory through creation is a common grace (extended to all), the *personal* knowledge of God that comes through the Bible is what makes revelation through creation more intimate—a means by which we can know God more.

I can't recall ever hearing a message when I was growing up about God's revelation through a knee, a tree, or a giant squid. Not once did I hear a sermon on the wildness of wolverines or the unique qualities of ice. When a preacher did mention creation, the reference was illustrative. I didn't hear that the very physical nature of creation could teach us something about the very nature of God. Of course, there were references to beauty and complexity in the cosmos, but I never heard anything about the physical nature of mountains, immune

systems, or gravitational waves saying something about what God is like.

I would have remembered a sermon like that. As I never heard one, I never imagined preaching one myself—until I got a letter from Vancouver's Regent College inviting me to participate in a John Templeton Foundation grant aimed at helping pastors explore the intersection of faith and science. Their letter stated that God speaks through two books and where those two books appeared to be in conflict, one of the books was not being properly read. I immediately accepted their invitation.

While the two-book idea had already taken significant root in my faith life by that point (leading me to preach dozens of sermons on God's revelation through music, film, art, sports, politics, and current events), I had never applied it to the sphere of science. Yet, if God speaks through the creation, how could we ever understand this physical text apart from the gift of science?

Science unpacks God's creation words. Scientists are made in the image of an empirical God. They think God's thoughts after God.[4] Everything that science explores was a thought in the mind of God before it ever came to be.[5] All physical reality has its genesis in God's imagination. God was the first physicist, chemist, and biologist. According to the Bible, Jesus was the means through which God made all things (John 1:1–3; Col. 1:15–17; Heb. 1:2). Jesus mediated both creation and salvation. The cosmos reflects Christ's world-arranging wisdom.

Science points to, reflects, and illuminates the mind of Christ. Even as the person and work of Jesus are mysteriously veiled in the Bible's Old Testament, the person and work of Jesus are also mysteriously veiled in the fabric of creation.

This mysterious connection makes me wonder if there is a deeper truth at play: Could it be that God has always meant for these two

books to be read *together*, in concert with one another, co-illuminating each other—the Bible shining light on creation and creation bringing deeper understanding to the Scriptures?

Is God's revelation this all-encompassing?

I wept the first time I read these thoughts on the matter from theologian Herman Bavinck:

> Revelation, while having its center in the person of Jesus Christ, in its periphery extends to the uttermost ends of creation.
>
> It does not stand isolated in nature and history, does not resemble an island in the ocean, nor a drop of oil upon water. With the whole of nature, with the whole of history, with the whole of humanity, with the family and society, with science and art it is intimately connected. The world itself rests on revelation; revelation is the presupposition, the foundation, the secret of all that exists in all its forms.
>
> The deeper science pushes its investigations, the more clearly it will discover that revelation underlies all created being. In every moment of time beats the pulse of eternity; every point in space is filled with the omnipresence of God; the finite is supported by the infinite, all becoming is rooted in being.
>
> Together with all created things, that special revelation that comes to us in the Person of Christ is built on these presuppositions. The foundations of creation and redemption are the *same*. The Logos who became flesh is the *same* by whom all things were made. The first-born from the dead is also the first-born of every creature. The Son, whom the Father made heir of all things, is the *same* by whom he also made the worlds.
>
> General revelation leads to special, special revelation points back to general. The one *calls for the other*, and without it

remains imperfect and unintelligible. *Together* they proclaim the manifold wisdom which God has displayed in creation and redemption [emphasis mine].[6]

Creation reveals things about the nature of God. God speaks through the cosmos. Creation is God's first book. To read it we need science. Science is not the enemy of the Christian faith; it's an ally!

JESUS AND THE NATURAL WORLD

Jesus referenced creation in many of His parables and teachings. He taught that the kingdom of God is like a seed, yeast, salt, birds, flowers, and the expanding nature of fermenting grapes. Jesus called Himself the light of the world, the true vine, a cornerstone, the root, and the bright and morning star. Often Jesus used nature to nudge His followers toward spiritual understanding, suggesting they consider the grass of the field, the solidity of rock, the shrewdness of snakes, the innocence of doves, the humility of a child, the technique of hens gathering their chicks, the germination of wheat kernels, the way the wind blows, the constancy of the sun, and the indiscriminate nature of rain.

> **Creation is God's first book. To read it we need science.**

On first reading, many of these nature references could be taken as mere figures of speech, but, if Jesus really is the one through whom all things were made, perhaps there is also a deeper meaning. When Jesus told His followers to "learn this lesson from the fig tree" (Matt. 24:32), was He cognizant of all the biological wisdom that went into conceiving that tree in the first place?

In the gospel of John, we read that Jesus clearly knew where He

came from (John 13:3). At one point He prayed, "Father, glorify me in your own presence with the glory that I had with you before the world existed" (John 17:5 ESV). Later He prayed, "Father, I want those you have given me to be with me where I am, and to see my glory, the glory you have given me because you loved me before the creation of the world" (John 17:24). Jesus clearly recalled the pre-creation glory He shared with the Father. His miracles imply an ongoing connection to His pre-incarnate power. If Jesus could recall His pre-creation glory in these ways, could He also recall all that He knew about the nature of a world that was made through Him? Was Jesus aware of the particle/wave nature of light when He said He was the light of the world?

Since Jesus knew that creation was made through Him, He would have known that "light" was made through Him, which gives His words a deeper meaning. Beyond being a good analogy, light is a good part of God's creation, made to operate in a certain way, and reflective of God's thinking and being. Of all created things, Jesus equated Himself with light.

No matter how specifically Jesus in His self-limiting omniscience (see Matt. 24:36) understood the scientific nature of light, His Father (whose will Jesus followed unerringly) certainly did. When Jesus called Himself the light of the world, God the Father knew *all that there is to know* about the science behind light.

The Father, who knows Jesus best, has a full knowledge of creation. For us to know more about Jesus, we need to know more about creation. Science helps us get there.

The Spirit who turns people's faces to God is the same Spirit who hovered over the face of the unformed cosmos. The Spirit who inspired the Bible is the same Spirit who brought light to the universe.

If we want to know the mind of Christ, we need to gain a deeper understanding of the physical nature of light (and of all creation).

We need to read biblical creation references with the Author's omniscience and original intent in mind.

To do that we need science.

THIS BOOK

Each chapter of this book begins with a story that connects a particular field of science or facet of nature with a unique attribute or characteristic of God (as known through the Bible). These stories are meant to capture moments of co-illumination—where God's truth via creation rhymes with or echoes God's truth via the Bible, and vice versa. The hope is that each connection will lead the reader into a deeper experience of God's omnipresence.

Physical truths unpacked by modern-day science resonate with ancient biblical truths.

By making these connections I am not claiming that the Bible contains all that science unpacks or that science points to all that the Bible reveals, but only that these two separate books seem to have a lot of co-illuminating overlap. If God is the author of both creation and the Bible, we can expect the truth in one text to echo with the other. While the Bible's earthly writers could never have foreseen a connection between their words and the words of creation (as unpacked by science), surely God could have. The same is true in the other direction. It is clearly within God's omniscient prerogative to have physical truths unpacked by modern-day science resonate with ancient biblical truths.

The scientists interviewed for this book come from various fields. Each chapter has a separate foreword written by a scientist with expertise in the field referenced in the chapter.

Each chapter of this book will also include theological reflection to help you better recognize God through the science you engage in your life—at your work, in your studies, or as you follow the news.

All the chapters (even this introduction) include a *lectio scientia*. This is a spiritual practice to help you engage God through science (even if you're not naturally scientifically oriented).

A PROPHETIC IMAGINATION

Through the prophet Isaiah, God says,

> "See, the former things have taken place,
>   and new things I declare;
> before they spring into being
>   I announce them to you." . . .
>
> "I am doing a new thing!" . . .
>
> "From now on I will tell you of new things,
>   of hidden things unknown to you.
> They are created now, and not long ago;
>   you have not heard of them before today.
> So you cannot say,
>   'Yes, I knew of them.'" **ISA. 42:9; 43:19; 48:7**

Even as Isaiah's contemporaries had trouble imagining what God had in store with the coming of Jesus, we are stretched to think that the Jesus we know through the Gospels can also be known through creation.

Theologian Walter Brueggemann writes, "If there is any point at which most of us are manifestly co-opted [by the commonly accepted

> **We need to believe that God can be known through creation in concert with the Bible.**

view of reality], it is in this way. We do not believe that there will be newness but only that there will be merely a moving of the pieces into new patterns."[7]

God can and will do something new. We need to trust and believe that God can be known through creation in concert with the Bible in an authoritative, epiphany-inducing, life-transforming, all-things-filling way.

Like Brueggemann, we need to ask "not whether it is realistic or practical or viable but whether it is imaginable."[8]

LECTIO SCIENTIA

The Spiritual Discipline of Scientific Knowing

In his classic book *Celebration of Discipline*, Richard Foster defines a spiritual discipline as a means through which ordinary people can enter into a deeper experience with God. At its core, a discipline is a spiritual practice where "the inner attitude of the heart is far more crucial than the mechanics."[9] In order to effectively engage God through a spiritual discipline there must be a "longing after God"[10]—a deep desire to know, understand, and experience God more.

What's true for the classical disciplines is also true for the discipline of *scientific knowing*. To know God through science, we need to *want* to know God through science. This desire, of course, is also a created thing—authored by a God who wants to be known through all things. To help make this happen, God created a compulsion in us to want God so deeply, so often, and by whatever means available that it would take something like revelation through creation to make

it happen. To help us engage the fullness of God, we've been given a huge revelatory book—creation.

To engage creation, we need to acknowledge that it speaks a different language than the Bible speaks—a seemingly infinite number of languages involving color, sound, complexity, scale, order, chaos, beauty, time, feeling, element, animal, and more. God uses all these languages to reveal Himself in a more all-encompassing way.

In his wonderful book *Ravished by Beauty*, theologian Belden Lane introduces the reader to many thinkers who have engaged the revelatory nature of creation deeply. Preeminent in his list of creation theologians is John Calvin. Calvin noted that "all creatures, from those in the heavens to those under the earth, are able to act as witnesses and messengers of God's glory. . . . For the little birds that sing, sing of God; the beasts clamor for him; the elements dread him, the mountains echo him, the fountains and flowing waters cast their glances at him . . . and the grass and flowers laugh before him."[11]

Christ speaks through the parable of creation so that, through everything, we can attend to Him and hear His voice (if we have eyes, ears, and hearts to see).

The question is do you want this?

Do you want to know God in this kind of creation-attentive way?

This question is crucial because a more fulsome experience of God can only come about through a more fulsome commitment on your part.

And where do you find the heart for that?

You ask for it.

PRAY

Lord God Almighty, Maker of heaven and earth, teach me how to attend to creation. Quicken my senses, kindle my imagination, and

reengage my mind. Free me from my spiritual dullness and revelatory sloth. Touch my eyes and ears and heart. Turn my mind to You, and take every thought captive to Your wisdom. Create a thirst in me that only You can slake. "As the deer pants for streams of water, so my soul pants for you, my God" (Ps. 42:1). Deepen my desire. Wake up my soul. Teach me how to attend to Your creational words.

PRACTICE

The next time a scientific truth catches your attention—via the news, through your work, or in your studies—stop and take note of how it makes you *feel*. Write that feeling down and ask how it makes you feel more *yourself*. If God made you to become more yourself (as you come to know God), then revelation through creation should help you know yourself more. As you begin to articulate the self-understanding that comes with this particular scientific truth, take note of any Bible passages or theological truths that come to mind. As they come to mind, let them shine a light on the creational truth you're engaging (and vice versa). As the co-illuminating conversation unfolds, continue to take note of how you're becoming more yourself.

When I first saw the Cassini Space Probe's image of earth as seen through Saturn's rings, I was dumbstruck. Seeing our planet from nine hundred million miles away was like getting a God's-eye view of our planet. The perspective made me feel tiny and transient, even as I felt elevated and honored to know the God who made our solar system. These feelings of insignificance and glory came together with the psalmist's words:

> When I consider your heavens,
>> the work of your fingers,
> the moon and the stars,

which you have set in place,
what is mankind that you are mindful of them,
human beings that you care for them?
You have made them a little lower than the angels
and crowned them with glory and honor. **PS. 8:3-5**

The Cassini image perfectly captured the psalmist's turn from "What is mankind that you are mindful of them?" to "You have made them a little lower than angels and crowned them with glory and honor." What a gift to be graced with an organization like NASA, to be able to send a probe to the outer reaches of our solar system, to know what we now know about Saturn's rings, and to know the God who conceived of it all! What the poet of Psalm 8 does through words, Cassini did through image—and God speaks through both.

This is the power of God's revelation through creation, engaging the whole of your being through all of your senses.

CHAPTER ONE

RADIATION THERAPY AND THE EMPIRICAL MIND OF GOD

A Word from Jacob Van Dyk

WORKING IN A CLINICAL, cancer-therapy environment, where science applications span multiple disciplines, including medicine, physics, biology, engineering technology, and computer science, a person gets to interact with people of multiple backgrounds with a variety of beliefs and faiths.

One of my close colleagues of many years, as well as being one of the very prominent medical physicists in the international scene and a recipient of the Order of Canada, has written in his autobiography, "I don't feel I have a religion, at least not in the sense of just accepting something that someone wrote down—someone who lived long ago and had much less knowledge about the world and the universe than we have. . . . Is there a God? Not of a personal kind anyway! If we are to have a good world, we have to make it so ourselves."[1] Another one of my professional colleagues, who also is well known for the foundational medical physics text that he has written, also wrote a book in his retirement, in search of his "scientific and religious view of creation." To quote, "The most difficult problem with all religions is their embrace of supernaturalism without question. God is

supernatural."[2] His conclusion: "Do not take a chance on blind faith. Do not take a shot in the dark. Use your head. If you are convinced in your mind that your religion is the correct one for you, then love it and cherish it. Call it a gift from your God."[3]

These are documented perspectives on faith and religion within my professional circles. Clearly, there are other perspectives. John Van Sloten writes elegantly here on science, radiotherapy, and the treatment of cancer. His starting point is that there is a God and that our experiences in our quest for advancing science, technology, and medicine reflect the mind of God. I have been raised from childhood in the Christian faith. I have struggled in my life with the understanding of God and how He influences my daily actions, my decision-making, and my shared life with my wife and children. I have reflected on many of the scientific arguments for and against the existence of God. I have concluded that science, on its own, cannot explain the origin of life. Thus, there must be a greater being who created life and the universe as we know it.

The Bible expands on this truth, both in the Old and New Testaments, with many facts shown to be historically correct. While that does not mean every word and concept are historically proven, or should be interpreted literally, it does demonstrate that a supreme being is involved in this world and in our personal lives. I, for one, feel very blessed.

I can look at my life and see influences that are expressions of a God who is involved. Whether other people would say that about their lives is a very open question. Certainly, there are circumstances in people's lives where individuals feel alienated and alone. To me there is no simple answer to these issues other

than that we live in a world impacted by complex circumstances as well as by our own decisions and actions.

So how do I see the mind of God in my professional domain? The world is ordered according to fundamental laws and physical, chemical, and biological processes. This created order reflects the mind of God. It is up to us as humans to uncover (or discover) this order to advance our knowledge. As our knowledge advances, we have the potential to reduce the impacts of ill-health and improve our quality of life. Each discovery, each advancement, each new technology, each improved diagnostic procedure, each new computer software package, each improved radiation treatment technique, each improved understanding of human biology, each positive clinical trial, provides another stepping stone in reflecting the makeup of this world and everything in it, which in turn reflects the mind of God.

Jacob Van Dyk, MSc, FCCPM, FAAPM, FCOMP, DSc (hon), is professor emeritus of Oncology, Medical Biophysics, Medical Imaging, and Physics and Astronomy at the Western University, London, Ontario, Canada. Dr. Van Dyk has won numerous teaching awards, published four radiation oncology textbooks, and was named one of the top fifty medical physicists "who have made an outstanding contribution to the advancement of medical physics over the last 50 years," according to the International Organization for Medical Physics. More recently, he has published another book, largely intended for a more general non-medical physics audience, entitled True Tales of Medical Physics: Insights into a Life Saving Specialty. *In 2022, he won the prestigious American Association of Physicists in Medicine Coolidge Gold Medal Award.*

1

RADIATION THERAPY AND THE EMPIRICAL MIND OF GOD

GOD knows what's going on.
He takes the measure of everything that happens.

1 SAMUEL 2:3 MSG

Several years ago, a woman with late-stage cancer approached me and suggested I preach a sermon on radiation physics. She'd been undergoing treatment and was fascinated by the technology. She saw it as a healing gift and wondered what radiation therapy could tell us about God. I was intrigued but also daunted by such a complex topic.

Later that same week I received an email from my friend Jake Van Dyk, who was in town and wanted to catch up. I knew he was a physicist but had no idea then that he'd literally written the book on radiation physics—*three* textbooks (at that time), actually. Perfect timing—he could help me with the science for my sermon, and I could introduce him to a new theological take on his work.

As we spoke about radiation therapy, I began to better understand the mind of a medical physicist (and a scientist in general). Jake had

always been good at physics and math in school and at any rationally structured course. A keen observer with a questioning curiosity, he wanted to know how things worked. He was organized, reasoned, and clear-thinking. To him, good science had to make a practical difference. His capacity to assess and measure came naturally—as did quantitative analysis. His well-developed ability to process large quantities of data enabled him to tackle complex questions. He took all the time needed to get to the right answer. He was good at seeing patterns. His love for teaching ranged from one-on-one interactions to writing textbooks. To Jake, knowledge was a gift to be shared. He loved research and analysis and wanted to do his part to help people with cancer and improve healthcare.

Engaging Jake's empirical aptitudes, I began to catch glimpses of the mind of God. God clearly understands how things work. Divine reason holds the cosmos together. God sees, measures, and knows and has an infinite capacity to process data, recognize patterns and make every connection. God is rational—and good at math.

When a scientific mind is fully itself in all these ways it reflects God's mind and—more than that—the scientific mind is close to its Maker. Physicist John Polkinghorne writes, "There is a remarkable congruence between the experienced rationality of our minds and the perceived rationality of the world around us."[4] Rational experiences, it seems, are made for a rational universe. When the two come together a scientist can experience the presence of God.

A scientist's gratification in discovering a pattern is connected to God's gratification in *creating* that pattern. The rational satisfaction of understanding how something works is akin to the rational satisfaction of having *made* that thing work. When science empirically engages a reality that was empirically conceived, it really does appear to be thinking God's thoughts after God. In those moments, the mind of the Maker can be rationally experienced.

Near the end of my conversation with Jake, my physicist friend, another facet of his work reminded me of Christ. A medical physicist stands between science and technology. They bring the two together, speak both languages, and enable a healing synergy. Hearing him describe the mediating nature of his work caused me to recall the mediating nature of Christ.

I asked Jake if he'd ever experienced Christ in that place of mediation—not morally or ethically but scientifically, rationally, or technologically. His simple answer was yes. Because he was convinced that God made everything, every time Jake learned something new, he thanked God. When the new information led to improved patient outcomes, Jake recognized the love of Christ at work.

I probed more deeply, asking Jake if he'd ever experienced the *empirical* mind of Christ in a rational, scientific moment. At first, he equated the word *experience* with an emotional engagement of God. I could tell that—as a scientist—this was not his primary means of engaging reality. But experience doesn't always have to be emotional. We spoke about recognizing Christ in rational ways, and Jake told me about a spiritual experiment he'd once tried. Years earlier he'd read a book titled *Space for God*, which suggested building into your schedule reminders of God's presence in your life.[5] Jake set his watch to beep every hour. Every time he heard the beep a Bible verse ran through his head, "Be still, and know that I am God" (Ps. 46:10). Wherever he was—in a meeting, at a hospital, or reviewing new technology—he would have a timely reminder of who was in charge. This simple experiment had a deep impact on his practice of faith.

God has filled every second of cosmic time with reminders. The Spirit moves everywhere. According to the Scriptures, the Spirit gives spiritual gifts to God's people, including wisdom and knowledge. In reference to Solomon's wisdom, the Bible says, "He could speak with authority about all kinds of plants, from the great cedar of Lebanon to

the tiny hyssop that grows from cracks in a wall. He could also speak about animals, birds, small creatures, and fish" (1 Kings 4:33 NLT).

Scientific wisdom is God's wisdom. When a scientist experiences an innately scientific moment—learning something new, noticing a pattern, designing an experiment that yields good results, or talking knowledgeably about plants—there is an opportunity to be still and know that God is God.

FROM RATIONAL TO RELATIONAL

If science images a rational God and scientists are made to empirically experience God in moments of rational resonance, what would those moments of resonance look like? How would an empirically oriented mind, engaging an empirically generated world, *experience* the empirical mind of God? What steps could one take to transform these science moments into God-knowing moments?

To start, you would need to take God's omnipresence seriously. If God is everywhere, then God is present to every rational scientific moment. If you believe in a personal God, then it's reasonable to conclude that God can be known in any given moment. The God of the Bible listens and speaks and can be spoken to and listened to. While the lines of communication are not what they used to be—our capacities to engage God fall short—they haven't fallen away completely. Since God is the author of both creation and the Bible, and since God makes revelation through creation clear through knowledge gained through biblical revelation, we should expect to see similarities between these two patterns.

The process of discovering these patterns might play out something like this:

A scientist is caught by something of interest and wonders how it

works. In that moment, believing in a personal God who is there, the scientist asks, "What is it that You already know about this, God?" This deferential stance affirms God's attending presence.

Then the scientific seeker creates a hypothesis—a tentative explanation for what he or she is observing, an explanation that will be tested and further researched by ongoing study. In generating such a hypothesis, scientists of faith are essentially saying, "I think this is what You've done, God." In that moment of faith, they open themselves up to a possibility. By opening themselves up to a possibility, they open themselves up to the possibility of glimpsing God.

Next, an experiment is designed that will, scientists hope, gather the best information possible. A scientific search is like a spiritual search; both are pursuing answers. With every experiment, science measures and tests what it thinks might be true. The empirical questions posed are akin to the faith questions the New Testament's seekers asked the incarnate Jesus: *Who are You? What is God like? How does God operate?* When these questions are posed in the lab however, they are addressed to the *Creator* Jesus.

> **As scientists discover something about the physical nature of the universe, they encounter the One who conceived of it in the first place.**

The scientists then gather and collate all the data—in their minds and on their hard drives. Like Jesus' followers (who observed what Jesus did, how God worked through Him, what His parables meant), the scientists take all they've observed (what this protein does, how this subatomic particle works, how this molecule responds) and compile and sort it. They try to make sense of all the information they've been presented with.

Then the scientists begin to notice a path, structure, or way of being. As they experience that "aha" moment, the pattern of their

thinking falls into sync with the pattern of Christ's thinking. As they come to know something about the physical nature of the universe, they encounter the One who conceived of it in the first place. The Creator is right there, with them, within them, before them, before the creation of the world.

Finally, the scientists test their conclusion. Knowing that truth stands up to scrutiny, they send their findings out for peer review (even as they understand their thesis will continue to be tested by further scientific experimentation). If, over time, their conclusions are communally affirmed, then their best understanding of God's "new scientific word" goes out to all the world. When this happens, the scientist's feeling of scientific satisfaction echoes the same eternal satisfaction God expressed when He declared over His creation, "It is good."

WHEN RADIATION THERAPY IMAGES GOD

Radiation therapy images God. Radiation therapy comes from the imaginations of image-bearing scientists, technologists, and health-care practitioners. God made their empirical minds, their passions to make the world a better place, and their capacities to get the job done. Whenever a tumor is eradicated, we can literally thank God. And if you look closely, you'll see that the nature of radiation therapy reveals something about the nature of God.

Radiation therapy is multi-disciplinary.[6] It brings science, technology, and medical practitioners together. It was one of the earliest sub-disciplines to use computers for dose calculations and imaging. Because of the influence of science, radiation therapy is one of the first medical disciplines to introduce clinical trials. Radiation therapy is built on physics, math, geometry, and biology.[7] It synergistically combines knowledge from each of these fields to wield the "invisible

knife"[8] of radiation treatment as precisely as possible. Without good technology, complex algorithms, a deep understanding of particle physics, or the practical sensibilities of a physician, radiation therapy could not do what it does.[9] When a field of medicine draws this broadly from what God has made, it points to the imaginative breadth of God's healing mind.

God draws from an infinite number of resources to heal brokenness. When we see the breadth of human ingenuity in the healthcare system come together, we're glimpsing something of the fullness of God's omniscient power. The psalmist wrote, "The earth is the LORD's, and everything in it, the world, and all who live in it" (Ps. 24:1). Everything in the Lord's earth includes physics, physiology, and linear-accelerator technology.

Another unique God-imaging facet of radiation therapy is its precise geo-spatial nature. "In its simplest form, the aim of radiation therapy is to cure the tumor without harming the patient."[10] Over the past few decades, science and medicine have worked with ever-increasing precision to irradiate tumors with minimal damage to surrounding healthy cells. The history of this field of medicine chronicles the development of better and better imagery (to identify the scope of the tumor) that then enables more focused radiation dosing.

When radiation therapy began, there was only 2D X-ray imagery. Then came 3D CT scanning followed by IMRT (intensity-modulated radiation therapy). Next came IGRT (image-guided radiation therapy) with imaging capacities built into the machines. And now 4D imaging has been developed, which adjusts the targeted radiation beam to work in time with a patient's breathing, keeping the treatment moving with the tumor. In the future there will be 5D imaging, which will take into account a patient's unique biology, watching how the individual reacts to treatment in real time and tailoring the treatment to a person's particular genetic

makeup. All this increasingly accurate dosing happens while the radiation beam rotates *around* the patient, to minimize collateral cell radiation exposure.[11]

When you glimpse the glory of all this empirical precision, it's hard not to fall to your knees. God sees what's wrong and treats the problem more precisely than the best radiation treatment imaginable—and does so with minimal collateral damage (despite our temporal sufferings).

Like the best imaging technology, God sees from every angle and dimension. When physics, math, computing, and biology come together in radiation therapy, we get a glimpse of the all-seeing mind of God described in Scripture: "God knows what's going on. He takes the measure of everything that happens" (1 Sam. 2:3 MSG).

Whenever physicists, software engineers, technologists, or physicians play their part in facilitating radiation therapy—using their empirical sensibilities to full capacity—they are doing the rational, restorative work of God in the world.

Through the God-imaging empirical actions of these scientists, a holy wisdom is moving—the work of a divine, rationally resonant Presence, a Presence who wants relationship as much as He wants the eradication of cancer. This is who Christ is. He drew near to us so we could draw near to God—with all our hearts, souls, minds, and vocational acts.

What's amazing is that God accomplishes this *in* us even as God works *through* us to help others. Through the body-renewing work of radiation therapy, God renews the minds and hearts of scientists, technologists, and doctors—enabling them to become more fully themselves. As technologies develop, we develop. Better science gives us more capacity to do better science and gives us more empirical resonance with which to engage the mind of God.

Again, the more we work to understand the mind of God, the

more we can be changed into God's likeness, making us more like Christ!

BUT CANCER KILLS

A few months after telling my friend with cancer that I was going to preach on radiation therapy, I sat beside her hospital bed and held her hand. Her treatments had been ineffective. Death was near. Praying for peace, we felt God in the room. God was in that room—mysteriously through the presence of the Spirit and practically through all the medical history and technology that made up the hospital we were in.

God uses science to heal, but science is limited. Like all created things, it falls short. Science cannot see perfectly or act with total precision. Only God is that perfect and precise. Only God can imagine the full scope of all that is needed to make all things well.

The beauty of experiencing God's empirical presence is that it comes with a big dose of hope: "This is what the LORD says, he who made the earth, the LORD who formed it and established it—the LORD is his name: 'Call to me and I will answer you and tell you great and unsearchable things you do not know'" (Jer. 33:2–3).

Jesus wants scientists to know how He thinks. He wants them to meet Him in the reasoning process. He wants them to know the mind of Christ—spiritually, ethically, and rationally.

> **When scientists attend to creation, they're listening to how Christ thinks.**

If all things were made through Jesus, then clearly Jesus is fluent in physics, chemistry, and biology. In a very real sense, these languages are His native tongue. When humanity engages them,

God's world-ordering mind can be known through our rationally comprehending nature.

When scientists attend to creation, they're listening to how Christ thinks.

Science rationally observes, asks the right questions, and draws reasonable conclusions based on the evidence. Science wants the truth, the whole truth, and nothing but the truth. It is precise, economic, well ordered, and efficient. Science is driven to get it right when it comes to understanding reality—a reality God already understands. Both God and science want our world to reach its potential. To enable this, God gave science an innate capacity to rationally think God's thoughts after God.

LECTIO SCIENTIA

Experiencing the Empirical Mind of Christ

This chapter asks, "How would an empirically oriented mind, engaging an empirically generated world, *experience* the empirical mind of God?" The response is a step-by-step scenario detailing how a scientist of faith might engage God more deeply.

What works for a scientist of faith can also work for any empirically minded person as they engage the ongoing work of science. Every empirically resonant moment that plays out in the news today is an opportunity for a rationally attentive Christian to experience the empirical mind of God.

PRACTICE

Consider engaging the steps science takes as an opportunity to know God more.

What if when you read of a scientist expressing interest in how something works, you say to yourself, "You already know how it works, God. By even wondering about the nature of reality, this scientist is giving evidence of You. You created empirical curiosity and attentiveness. Their passion points to You."

When you hear a scientist describe how they went about generating their hypothesis (their questions and hoped-for answers), let the moment be a reminder of a God whose thoughts are not your thoughts, whose ways are above your ways. In humble incredulity, acknowledge the deeply insightful, prophetic nature of science, which raises questions most of us would never know to ask.

Acknowledge that even as God surely smiles when scientists better understand and appreciate the world, God also smiles when any of us better understand *any* facet of reality—relational, artistic, educational, or economic. Whenever we better understand how things work, God is glorified (whether we glorified Him on purpose or not). When science knows more through *its* means of truth-seeking, we can be encouraged to know God more through *all* means of truth-seeking. Science's constant questioning gives us permission to question.

As you take note of how science follows the data—accumulating it and discerning patterns—be reminded that you can observe your life in a similar way. Based on the evidence, life is often much better than we give it credit for. Whenever we consider what we're thankful for, we realize a surprising truth: life is mostly good most of the time. When science follows the data in a trustworthy way and discerns a true pattern, let it be a reminder of what is trustworthy and true in your life—God's good and greater pattern.

You can even learn to trust God through science's failures. Even with all our advances, science still falls painfully short. People die of cancer. Discoveries are used for nefarious purposes like atomic bombs or eugenics. Healthcare is commoditized, putting profits over people.

Researchers hoard their data or hide it behind paywalls. Competition undermines cooperation. Like all of humanity, science's sinful propensities remind us of the still-unhealed brokenness of our human condition.

Through the Old Testament prophet Isaiah, God said,

> "For my thoughts are not your thoughts,
>> neither are your ways my ways,"
>>> declares the LORD.
> "As the heavens are higher than the earth,
>> so are my ways higher than your ways
>> and my thoughts than your thoughts." **ISA. 55:8-9**

Isaiah's words are true in terms of what science can claim to empirically know about the nature of reality. They're also true in terms of the nature of human hearts. God's ways are beyond ours. God sees the whole picture, from all eternity. Our Maker's plan, based on the patterns of Scripture and creation and the ever-evolving gift of science, is to one day make all things new, to have a world where everyone knows God through all things. Centuries of scientific advances fit within this greater plan. If we can stand back far enough, the pattern will become clear.

Imagine engaging God through all the steps that make up the scientific method. Next time you read a compelling science news story, look past the empirical details to see the Empirical Mind behind the story. Go deeper. Let the empirical Spirit of Christ lead the way.

PRAY

Lord, give me eyes to see Your mind reflected in the mind of a scientist. Help me recognize the patterns You've put in place. Connect my reason to Yours. Make me curious for You. Be the answer to all my questions.

CHAPTER TWO

SUPERNOVAE AND GOD'S PASSION FOR MATTER

A Word from Deborah Haarsma

I LOVE JOHN VAN SLOTEN'S approach to creation. Many theologians have described Scripture and nature as two books of God's revelation, but John digs deep into this truth. He actively reads the two books together, with "the Bible shining light on creation and creation bringing deeper understanding to the Scriptures."[1] John draws fascinating examples from many fields of science and medicine. He then calls us to not only consider them intellectually, but to ponder them in our hearts and turn in worship to the Author of it all.

God delights in matter. God creates the elements of matter from other matter, mainly in the cores of stars and in supernova explosions. God builds up His creation in ever increasing layers of complexity into a universe of stars, nebulae, and galaxies, and ultimately life on earth and our own bodies.

God could just snap His fingers to make new carbon atoms, and they would appear from nothing. God is sovereign, and nothing prevents Him from doing that! Yet when we look at the universe, we see God choosing to do something different. He

chooses to make matter from matter, coming alongside and working with what He has already made. Before making a carbon atom, He has already made the helium atoms, as well as the stars in which they are found, the laws of physics governing nuclear fusion, and the fabric of space and time itself. Rather than overriding those previous creations, God works with them to accomplish His purposes and create new carbon atoms. This is not an efficient process; much helium remains behind. Nor is it a fast process; the fusion reactions themselves are quick, but the dispersal of the carbon from the dying star and its collection later in a new planet takes eons. Yet God doesn't take the shortcut. He chooses to work at the pace of His creation to make the elements.

That actually reminds me of Jesus Christ in His work on earth. The second member of the Trinity, through whom the stars were made, also walked in the dust of Palestine, shepherding His disciples. Can we see parallels? I see one in the way Jesus worked with His disciples, in commissioning them to be His witnesses. Jesus not only makes matter from matter but makes disciples from disciples. Jesus comes alongside the followers He already has, and rather than overriding them, He works with them to build the church. He could have snapped His fingers to make new disciples, and they would have appeared throughout the world. But He chose to do something different. He knew it would be an imperfect process—not efficient and not fast. Yet He put the future of the church into the hands of some rather imperfect disciples, and He puts it into our hands. He works by the power of His Spirit, working in us and through us to accomplish His purposes. He delights in making new matter, and He delights

in making new people. He works not only through dramatic miracles but in slow processes with what He has already made. The one who walked in the dust of Palestine is also the Creator of the Cosmos.

Dr. Deborah Haarsma is an astronomer and the president of BioLogos. She has studied large galaxies, galaxy clusters, the curvature of space, and the expansion of the universe, using telescopes around the world and in orbit. She is a frequent speaker and author on science and faith, including contributions to the books Four Views on Creation, Evolution, and Intelligent Design (Zondervan) and Christ and the Created Order (Zondervan). She wrote the book Origins (Faith Alive) with her husband and fellow physicist, Loren Haarsma, and edited the anthology Delight in Creation: Scientists Share Their Work with the Church (Center for Excellence in Preaching) with Rev. Scott Hoezee.

2

SUPERNOVAE
AND GOD'S PASSION
FOR MATTER

*He determines the number of the stars
and calls them each by name.*

PSALM 147:4

Several years ago, I attended a conference where I heard an astronomer give a talk on what the nature of the universe says about God. The lecture was beautifully illustrated with breathtaking Hubble Space Telescope images. The speaker clearly possessed a deep faith and understanding of the cosmos. While most attendees left the talk inspired, I left a little disappointed. I kept waiting for the moment when I'd hear something about how a particular facet of the nature of the universe illuminated a particular characteristic of God.

When it was time for Q&A, I raised my hand and asked what the universe uniquely says about the nature of God. The response, after a short pause, was "God is patient." This is a great truth, of course, but I had been hoping for more. At this point in my faith-and-science journey, I had begun to notice how some scientists of faith tended to

experience God via creation mostly through the broader categories of awe and wonder. These are important ways for engaging God (especially in relation to something as immense as the universe), but often scientists seemed to stop at this initial faith response. What truths would they uncover if they pushed beyond awe and wonder?

When I shared some my frustration with another conference attendee, a physics professor and Mars Rover researcher, she understood. She told me a little about what the nature of the universe has taught her about the nature of God. As she spoke, my heart brightened. This is what I was hoping to hear!

THE DEATH AND RESURRECTION OF MATTER

In the beginning God created the heavens and the earth. Out of nothing God made everything. God brought the universe into being in a very specific way.

According to the Mars Rover researcher I met, in the beginning,

> Only hydrogen, helium, and a little lithium were created—not nearly enough elements for life, as we know it, to exist. Heavier and more complex elements came about through the life and death of stars—two kinds, low-mass stars and high-mass stars. When a low-mass star dies, the element carbon is produced. When a high-mass star starts to die, elements like oxygen, neon, magnesium, and so on up the periodic table until you reach iron, are produced. Then, when a high-mass star explodes in a supernova, elements heavier than iron are made. The heavier elements that make us up are created in the end stages of a high-mass star's life. It is only through the death of these stars that the elements for life are created.[2]

According to the Bible, Jesus authored all of this process. He's the One through whom the universe was made (Heb. 1:2). Every element, birthed through every one of the estimated forty supernovae that explode every second in our known universe, was made through Him.[3] Matter came into being through the cosmos-arranging wisdom of Christ. In a very real sense, the dying and resurrecting Jesus of the Gospels created a dying and resurrecting universe. Through the life-and-death cycle of stars, He made more out of matter—more elements to fill the universe via supernovae and more *out of* those elements via all that they came to be, including His very own human body.

Jesus' physical body was formed from the stardust He made.

MATTER MATTERS

Clearly matter matters to Jesus—so much so that He took on a physical body. That body then went through life, death, resurrection, and ascension. That means Jesus' resurrected human body remains a part of the community of the Trinity. Is there a more powerful way for God to affirm that matter matters?

When Christ took on human nature, He also took on many of the heavier elements in the universe that form our bodies. So, through His death, resurrection, and ascension, Jesus really did make *all things* new (Rev. 21:5).

In the beginning, when the heavens and the earth were created, "God saw all that he had made, and it was very good" (Gen. 1:31). I wonder if now, when the Father sets His eyes on His embodied Son with all those universal elements held perfectly together in Him, He feels that same way. I wonder if when science proclaims its "very good" verdict on the physical nature of the universe—through how it values material reality and deems it worth studying—it is giving

> **Matter matters because it came from the mind of God.**

evidence to the heart and mind of a matter-loving God.

Matter matters because it came from the mind of God. God imagined, designed, and created the universe. The cosmos is God's brainchild. Matter also matters because it says something about who God is. The sheer quantity and complexity of matter is indicative of the immense scope of God's revelation. When science does what science does, it helps humanity unpack God's revelation through creation and affirms that science-loving human beings are made in the image of a creation-loving God.

MAKING MORE OUT OF MATTER

Another sign of just how much matter matters to God is matter's potential to become more.

Late in the life of a star, three helium atoms fuse to make carbon. Carbon is crucial for life. By fusing three helium atoms through the intense heat and pressure at the core of a star, they become more. For eons, Jesus has been making more out of matter in this way. Long before He was raised with His new, glorified, resurrected body, Jesus was prefiguring God's death and resurrection plan through the making-more-of-matter nature of the universe.

God's plan in Christ is to make all things new (Rev. 21:5). God made more out of helium atoms long before any of us carbon-based beings were here. God continues to make more out of matter by way of all the new things science brings into being. For all we know, God's plan may be to make more out of matter forever. Newness may not

be a one-time, static thing—which means we may be engaging in science for a long time.

When science makes more out of physical matter—for example, in a chemistry lab—it carries on an ancient tradition and lays the groundwork for an eternally new future. When those who work in science contribute to the making-more process, they participate in God's cosmic plan for the universe—working with and through God.

If matter matters this much and has this much innate potential, and if God uses science to reveal and unpack it all, then surely God can be known through many facets of science's valuing, studying, and making-more processes.

MATTER CONTINUES

When three helium atoms fuse to create carbon, their original nature continues in a new form. Whenever science makes more out of matter, some of what previously existed endures. The same is true when God takes what already exists and makes more out of it.

We see this happening in an ultimate sense through the resurrection body of Jesus. When His disciples first saw Him, "None of the disciples dared ask Him, 'Who are you?' They knew it was the Lord" (John 21:12). While His physical form had been transformed and glorified, He was still recognizable as *Jesus*.

Regarding the nature of our resurrected bodies, theologian Gordon Spykman writes,

> We do not know with full clarity "what we shall be"; but we do know that "when [Christ] appears we shall be like him, for we shall see him as he is" (1 John 3:2). . . . For "just as there is continuity between the seed and the plant, so there will

be continuity between the present body and the resurrection body." Yet, "just as one cannot tell from the appearance of the seed, what the future plant will look like, so we cannot tell by observing the present body exactly what the resurrection body will be like."[4]

Even as God made helium with the potential to become carbon and carbon with the potential to become a body, God has made us—our mortal flesh—with the potential to become, one day, eternal. Even as the disciples were able to see Jesus for who He really is, others will see us for who we really are. We'll be fully ourselves for the very first time.

We'll be made new.

We'll be *more*.

Every time nature makes more out of matter, we have a reminder of this glorious truth.

God has always been a making-more-out-of-things kind of God. In the Scriptures, Jesus' redemption story is prefigured through the ancient exodus story. Several old covenants preceded the new covenant in Christ. These covenants didn't disappear. Jesus said it Himself, "Do not think that I have come to abolish the Law or the Prophets; I have not come to abolish them but to fulfill them. For truly I tell you, until heaven and earth disappear, not the smallest letter, not the least stroke of a pen, will by any means disappear from the Law until everything is accomplished" (Matt. 5:17–18).

When science affirms how matter is renewed, humanity is given a pointer to God's cosmic renewal plan.

Even as the early creation elements of hydrogen, helium, and lithium have continued to this very day, they'll continue for all eternity

in some new and glorified form. From the beginning God has been foreshadowing this world-renewing, covenant-keeping plan through the Bible and creation. Again, when science affirms how matter is renewed, humanity is given a pointer to God's cosmic renewal plan.

Theologian Jürgen Moltmann wrote that because God's Spirit fills creation, "it is . . . possible to experience God *in, with and beneath* each everyday experience of the world."[5] This includes every scientific experience. Every facet of material reality *already* has something to say about who God is. As Moltmann writes, "In everything God is waiting for us."[6]

GOD DELIGHTS IN MATTER

Psalm 104 paints a beautiful picture of both the psalmist's and God's delight in creation:

Praise the LORD, my soul.

LORD my God, you are very great;
you are clothed with splendor and majesty.

The LORD wraps himself in light as with a garment;
he stretches out the heavens like a tent
and lays the beams of his upper chambers on their waters.
He makes the clouds his chariot
and rides on the wings of the wind.
He makes winds his messengers,
flames of fire his servants.

He set the earth on its foundations;
it can never be moved. **PS. 104:1-5**

The psalm goes on to name the glories of watery depths, mountains, thunder, springs, ravines, wild beasts, plants, birds, moon, and the sun. In a talk on this psalm, Dr. Richard Mouw notes that human beings aren't mentioned until almost halfway through the thirty-five verses of this Hebrew poem.[7] Clearly there was enough creational glory to be celebrated beyond and before that of human beings. Mouw applied this humbling observation to the question of why God took so much time to create the universe. Perhaps, like the psalmist, God wanted to celebrate and delight in the goodness of *all* creation.

Were the psalmist to have known about astrophysics, perhaps he might have also written:

> Gather together, all you elements;
>> hydrogen, lithium, and helium.
> For the Lord your God speaks;
>> fuse and be transformed.
> Give birth to carbon;
>> fill the cosmos with life.
> For you are mine;
>> you belong to me, says the Lord.

Science is only beginning to understand all that fills the cosmos. It may take an eternity to fully understand all that has been made. Perhaps humanity, along with God, will be delighting in the unending wisdom of creation forever.

Matter matters this much.

Making Matter Matter More

PRACTICE

If you were to write a psalm about creation, what would it look like?

Have you ever imagined how God feels about that one part of creation that really captures your heart?

When I wrote the psalm-like lines at the end of this chapter, I was overwhelmed by the thought that God might feel this way about this part of creation. Imagining God's delight in creation makes my delight in creation feel a lot more personal. I sensed a deep and intimate presence as I wrote those few phrases.

What if you tried to do it too?

What if, the next time you read something interesting about the nature of nature, you took what caught your attention and spent some time studying it and learning more about it? After understanding it more, what if you tried to imagine how God feels about that same created thing? You might try writing a few words in relation to the created thing you're pondering.

Do your research and then read Psalm 104 a few times (to get the cadence and poetry of the ancient text). Then try writing a few poetic lines.

Don't be intimidated. While we can't put words in God's mouth, we are made in the image of an imaginative God and we can reflect Him. As you follow the scientifically reasoned understanding in relation to what you're considering, let that reasoning be a teacher. Even as a scientist's mind follows after God's, let your mind follow after God.

Then write your own addendum to Psalm 104.

PRAY

God, I believe You made all things and that everything matters deeply to You. What I notice and find intriguing in creation is that You are already aware of its mysteries. Before I even see something new, You saw it. Let me see what You see, Lord. Heal my eyes and make them new. Transform my perceptions in relation to You and what You've made. Sync my thoughts with Yours and inspire my words, I pray.

CHAPTER THREE

ENGAGING GOD'S PROVIDENCE THROUGH KNEES AND FOSSILS

A Word from Laurie Hiemstra

I FIRST MET JOHN VAN SLOTEN at a church social event—
one that took place, quite apropos, at the Telus Spark Science
Centre in Calgary, Alberta.

I had been a church member prior to moving west to Banff
and was joining friends for a special day and church service
at the Dome Theatre at the Science Centre. I introduced myself,
and John's eyes lit up when he heard I was a knee surgeon.
Inwardly, I groaned. Likely I was about to hear about his newest
ache or pain, be regaled about his prior surgeries, or hear a re-
quest to help gain access to an overloaded healthcare system.
Instead, the conversation was one that changed many things for
me; he asked me to help him write a sermon about knees.

Having attended Calvin University in Grand Rapids,
Michigan, I was not new to the concept that God and science
were not at odds—that God speaks through science, and
science reveals God's sovereignty over creation. Yet I had not
fully appreciated how my career and my faith were integrated
in ways beyond simply being in a "helping" profession. By
restoring someone to function, we are participating in a miracle.

It is a step toward restoring creation to what God intended. As Johann Diemer says in his lecture "Nature and Miracle":

> Whenever the original law of Christ is restored, we see miraculous potentialities emerge as the elements are withdrawn from the destructive power and influence of sin and are led anew in their proper courses. . . . Through the signs and wonders the disintegrating power of sin is broken and its results overcome. What occurs is not a supernatural interference in the positive consequence of a natural process but a fully natural interference in the negative consequence of a sinful process.[1]

In this chapter, John Van Sloten takes the job of a surgeon and relates it to the providence of God. When the job of restoring a knee, or a person, to full active function aligns with God's will, He works through us to achieve His purpose. There is more to being a surgeon than helping people, or being kind, or being the best we can be. We are image bearers of God, the conduit that allows God to intervene in creation in accordance with His will and for His people to know God through what He has made.

Dr. Laurie Hiemstra is an orthopedic surgeon, Banff Sport Medicine, and associate professor at the University of Calgary. She is the director of research at the Banff Sport Medicine Foundation, which has completed seventy publications and currently has more than thirty clinical projects underway. Dr. Hiemstra is the 77th president of the Canadian Orthopaedic Association.

3

ENGAGING GOD'S PROVIDENCE THROUGH KNEES AND FOSSILS

Who can speak and have it happen
if the Lord has not decreed it?

LAMENTATIONS 3:37

Years ago, I sat down to read British physicist and theologian John Polkinghorne's book *Science and the Trinity*.[2] By the time I got to page 5, every synapse in my brain was firing in epiphany.

Polkinghorne writes about the challenge of reconciling the belief that God providentially intervenes in the world with the claim that science already explains how everything works. If science shows us that the universe is self-sustaining and doesn't need God's help, how could providential intervention ever work in a universe based on the unchangeable laws of nature?

Polkinghorne addresses this paradoxical challenge in two ways—by arguing that science doesn't know as much as it claims and that human intervention into the physical nature of the universe makes room for the possibility of God's interventions.

Polkinghorne also notes that modern physics now recognizes the *unpredictable* nature of our universe. Quantum theory and chaos theory change the "merely mechanical account of physical process" that used to be the foundation of science.[3] The universe is more open-ended than we thought. In Polkinghorne's words, nature has a "divinely ordained open grain" (an accessibility) that leaves room for the possibility of human intervention.[4]

Polkinghorne adds that if human beings can "act as agents in the world . . . it would not seem reasonable to deny the possibility of some analogous capacity in the Creator."[5] If human beings can intervene in and shape an accessible universe, then surely God can as well.

Intervening scientists, therefore, may themselves be the strongest proof for the possibility of a providentially intervening God. Though scientists or medical professionals can't themselves work miracles, scientific interventions seem directly linked to divine interventions. God works through scientific interventions.

Could it be that when a chemist creates a new molecule or a neuroscientist a new drug or a surgeon a new knee, *God* is providing a new molecule, drug, or knee?

If God works through the providential interventions of science, perhaps these interventions—by their very nature—can teach us about how God intervenes. If God does providentially intervene through science, then good scientific interventions have something to say about who God is.

A KNEE SURGEON

I first experienced this phenomenon through a conversation I had with knee surgeon Dr. Laurie Hiemstra. As a Christian, she had always understood that her faith and work were connected, and she

demonstrated this by attentively caring for her patients. But when I sent Laurie a list of questions designed to elicit a deeper awareness of the providentially intervening nature of her work, her view of God at work changed. She began to realize that her surgical interventions imaged God's providential interventions. Poring over her ten-page response, I knew that the door to a deeper experience of God at work had been opened.

The human knee is both a simple and complex joint. Its complexity lies in subtle things. The joint cannot function on its own and needs menisci, muscles, ligaments, and a nervous system. The knee does not have much inherent bony stability, yet the forces it absorbs to do things, like pivoting during an athletic activity, are impressive. Bones supply the most stability to a joint; they are strong and difficult to break. With minimal bony structure, the stability of the knee is enhanced by the soft tissue structures contained in and around it. When you're standing, knees bear the entire weight of your body. The strain increases to three times your body weight when you're walking and up to five or six times your body weight when you're jumping or landing. These are enormous forces on a structure with minimal bony stability. This means that the soft tissues (the ligaments, menisci, etc.) have a huge role to play in the ability of the knee to move and function.[6]

Dr. Hiemstra loves being a knee specialist. While early in her career she worked on many joints, she now works on only this one. To understand the intricacies of the knee more fully, she needed to give it her full attention. This attention gives her a greater capacity to deal with more complex problems. Here's how she describes one moment of surgical flow:

> When I am performing a new surgery that no one in the
> country has done before, and it is all going according to plan,

say a trochleoplasty, I come prepared. I travel to Europe and do a two-week fellowship to learn the procedure. I practice in the cadaver lab. I watch all the videos on the internet. I am prepared—over-prepared maybe. I know I have the skill and knowledge to do the surgery, but it is new, cutting edge. There is no long-term experience in Canada; I am the first person to do it. I have stressed about it—and then it turns out to be easier than I thought. Surgery is a lot like sport. You practice, you visualize, you meditate, you prepare. Despite that, the unexpected can always happen. This is when the training kicks in, and you have confidence. You know you have trained well, prepared well. When you are prepared and experienced like that, you anticipate the problems and prevent them from happening. My students always wonder how I can make a surgery look so easy. . . . With experience, you do these things without even thinking about it.[7]

This moment of surgical flow has a connection to God. Like the most qualified surgeon, God also does new things and is always prepared. God has all the requisite skills and knowledge to effectively do the job. God anticipates the unexpected and makes it look easy. With an eternity's worth of experience, God can do things without even thinking about it.

When I shared these connections with Dr. Hiemstra, she realized her relationship with her students echoes God's relationship with her.

Through her training and experience, Dr. Hiemstra was able to hone her skills and image an all-knowing God more fully. In the fullness of these image-bearing moments, she began to understand how her providentially intervening work was concurrent with God's.

God can be known through good interpersonal interactions with patients, but He can also be known through the mechanics of what

a surgeon does—through well-trained hands connected to a well-trained mind. God wants to be known in these places. The minds and hands of surgeons are made to resonate with God's mind and "hands." A surgeon's providential intervention into the biomechanics of the human knee really is akin to God's providential intervention. The surgeon's experience of knowing and doing things so well that they don't have to think about them is a pointer to the kind of freedom with which God exercises world-saving power. The foresight that comes with a doctor's extensive knowledge of her specialty is a foretaste of God's omniscience.

When a concurrent experience of God through surgical intervention engages the profound complexity (and accessibility) of a human knee—with its capacity to have new grooves carved into bones, ligaments repurposed, and receptivity to bio-absorbable interference screws—the knowing of God through the phenomenon of surgery goes deeper. Even as the most skilled surgeon can complete a complex surgery and enable the greatest of recoveries, so too does God intervene in the most broken of circumstances to make all things new.

PERFECT IN UNIQUENESS, BEAUTY, AND FUNCTION

To help unpack the nature of the knee, I asked Dr. Hiemstra what she as a surgeon found most compelling about the joint—what made it unique, beautiful, and so perfectly functional.

Because she had studied and repaired it for years, Dr. Hiemstra knew the knee's complexities, its strengths and weaknesses, and its possible restoration after damage. As I engaged her understanding of the knee, I began to learn something about the nature of God. The surgeon described the knee's lack of bony stability and its necessary

reliance on soft tissue. This seemingly vulnerable design, however, was just right in terms of allowing the knee to pivot, to absorb extraordinary loads, and to enable running. I found myself considering a God who took the seemingly vulnerable approach of giving humanity free will, choosing vulnerability over the rigidity of fixing our choices so that we can have full, free, and able lives. In order to choose God, we need to be able to pivot.

When Dr. Hiemstra described how the knee is lubricated only through use, I was reminded of how a life of faith is meant to be an active one. As she described how the knee was made for movement, I realized it was designed by a God who moves. Everything in the cosmos is designed by a God who moves.

My mind and spirit quickened with interest as each unique facet the doctor described about the knee remined me of a unique facet of the nature of God. Because I can know how God moves through the Bible, I was able to recognize patterns in how God moves in the biomechanics of the knee. God's physiological words rhymed and resonated with God's biblical words. In those resonant moments I had a sense that God was present—in the same way artists are present through their paintings.

As an expert on the knee, Dr. Hiemstra resonated with God's physiological words; her mind was already connecting her work with certain Bible passages and theological truths about God. Dr. Hiemstra quoted the Lord's Day 1 from the Heidelberg Catechism, describing a God who watches over us in such a way that not a hair can fall from our heads outside of God's will and how all things must work together for our salvation.[8] She quoted Psalm 8:4: "What is mankind that you are mindful of them, human beings that you care for them?" and Psalm 100:3, "Know that the LORD is God. It is he who made us, and we are his." She pointed out the God who restores described in Isaiah 40:31: "But those who hope in the LORD will

renew their strength. They will soar on wings like eagles; they will run and not grow weary, they will walk and not be faint."

While Dr. Hiemstra had engaged God's voice through these words from the catechism and the Bible, she was beginning to also engage them through the physiological nature of the knee. God's word through creation was echoing and affirming God's written Word.

Dr. Hiemstra and I discussed the providentially concurrent nature of her work—that is, how God provided for the patient as she provided for the patient. All kinds of connections emerged when I asked what she loved about being a knee surgeon and in what ways that love was like God's. Just as she loves the way our knees enable us to move and values the simplicity, vulnerability, and hidden complexity of the joint, we know God the Designer delights in His own creative work. God is honored when a surgeon specializes and shares God's deep knowledge of the knee and when that surgeon brings healing power and wisdom to bear in restoring mobility.

> **God's word through creation was echoing and affirming God's written Word.**

When you articulate what you love about your work, you name what God loves about your work. Where your passion is, that's where providential concurrence happens. When a surgeon clearly names what she loves doing, she is nearer to seeing and experiencing God in that moment of flow.

Moments of flow are one of the best ways to begin engaging God's presence. When you are completely focused and totally engrossed in what you are made to do, time seems to disappear and you are most yourself. You can fully recognize and settle into your image-bearing nature and attributes. Knowing your nature and attributes helps you know *God's* nature and attributes, which then creates a cycle of knowing.

This is what God has made human beings for—to know God in all things.[9] Science helps us unpack God's wisdom as revealed in the natural world. The God who providentially intervenes in creation wants to be known through the creation-intervening work of science. In a very real sense, science images God as it continues to shape God's world. One day, when the work of science is in perfect sync with God's providential will, we will come to know God more fully—as we're meant to.

PROVIDENCE DEFINED

A deeper understanding of the theological nature of providence can help us better understand how God works in connection with human beings as they work.

According to the Bible, God is a hands-on Creator and caregiver. God actively creates, sustains, preserves, and guides all things to their ultimate fulfillment. John Calvin taught, "As keeper of the keys, [God] governs all events. Thus [providence] pertains no less to his hands than to his eyes."[10] God is involved with creation. Gordon Spykman said, "Where God's creating activity leaves off, there his providential care takes over. These two phases . . . are inextricably interconnected. Providence presupposes creation . . . creation moves on naturally and directly into providence, with no gap in between."[11]

Creation and providence are connected—and not just chronologically. God built sustaining care into the very design of the universe. It's woven into the very fabric of the cosmos.

All the mechanisms that hold the universe together are, according to the apostle Paul, held together in Jesus: "For in him all things were created: things in heaven and on earth, visible and invisible, whether thrones or powers or rulers or authorities; all things have

been created through him and for him. He is before all things, and in him all things hold together" (Col. 1:16–17). Yet the line between the care God *built into* creation and the care God brings through *ongoing providence* can be a blurry one.

God cares for a world that's already cared for. God feeds all creatures by way of an ecosystem's innate life-sustaining structures. God keeps our feet on the ground by a natural gravitational pull. Much of God's providence, it seems, is built in.

God's ongoing interventions play out in the context of an already self-sustaining world. Perhaps this is why so many scientific interventions seek to follow the existing grain of the cosmos—with new cancer treatments seeking to engage existing immune systems and new structures for the knee following after existing structures. More than most of us, scientists know they are caring for a world that already has a great capacity to care for itself. Knowingly or not, science images God when its providential interventions respect and go with the created grain of the cosmos.

When scientists choose to go with the grain of the cosmos, could it be that they are aligning their thoughts with the *Creator* of the cosmos? This image-bearing activity can give us a glimpse of the mind of God.

When God providentially intervenes, this doesn't necessarily override nature's laws or our free wills. Providence is bigger than that. Jesuit theologian Karl Rahner suggests that human beings are most autonomous when they are *most* dependent on God. God made humans to fully depend on God, and gives us free will to choose that dependence. When we do, we are in the place where our wills were made to be. True autonomy increases in the same proportion as dependence on God.[12] When free will falls in line with God's will, we become truly free.

What could this mean for those whose work regularly intervenes with and shapes nature? If God is an intervening God who holds everything in creation, then surely God *is* at work in all the good that

science pursues. Even as those who work in science give evidence to the possibility of God's providential intervention, they also open the door to understanding *how* a providentially intervening God works.

CONCURRENCE

One way that God providentially works is through a phenomenon called *concurrence* where "the same deed is in its entirety both a deed of God and a deed of the creature. It is a deed of God insofar as it is determined from moment to moment by the will of God. And it is a deed of man insofar as God realizes it through the self-activity of the creature."[13] Or, as it says in Proverbs, "In their hearts humans plan their course, but the LORD establishes their steps" (Prov. 16:9).

Concurrence is a perplexing mystery, but sometimes we uncover clues into how it works—when two scientists on opposite sides of the planet unknowingly make the same discovery at the same time; when a researcher's experiment goes terribly wrong, but her results open up a promising new field of inquiry; when a paleontologist sits on a rock while on holiday and serendipitously notices what appear to be ancient human footprints embedded in the stone.[14]

Could concurrent discoveries be signs of a concurrently present and active God? Even as two scientists unknowingly make the same discovery, could each of these scientists be working concurrently with God?

Could human failures (once the retrospective lesson is learned) be affirmations of God's providential direction? Could paleontological steps be pointers to a world-establishing God?

Paleontologist Neil Shubin writes that some of the best places to look for fossilized bones are those where you walk for miles over bare bedrock. You may encounter areas where bones are "weathering out."

Because fossilized bones are harder than the rock they are embedded in, they erode at a slower rate and protrude from the rock surface. This density variation is why many discoveries happen in desert areas like the Sahara or in Greenland. Shubin adds, "This all sounds very logical, but let's not forget serendipity. . . . Our first important discoveries didn't happen in a desert, but along a roadside in central Pennsylvania where the exposures could hardly have been worse. To top it all off, we were looking there only because we did not have much money."[15]

AN ACCESSIBLE UNIVERSE

Even as God moves in concurrent ways through the intervening endeavors of science, God moved in making a world that is physically accessible in terms of both its nature and timing.

Fossils in the bedrock are accessible because God has been clearing the ground of ice and soil through natural erosion for thousands of years. By establishing a fossilization process in which the density of bones-turned-to-stone is slightly higher than the surrounding rock, God is whispering, "Hey, look here!" When God uses budget shortfalls and scheduling limitations alongside solid scientific analysis to lead a team to just the right roadside in Pennsylvania, God is proven a trustworthy guide.

As Polkinghorne noted, God's universe is accessible.[16] For providence to effect change, nature has to be *open* to its intervention. Protons must be controllable (to a degree) so that we can fly them in circles at nearly the speed of light in the Large Hadron Collider to try to figure out how matter came to be. The human body's wound-healing mechanisms must dependably allow for the intervention of scalpel and suture so recovery from open-heart surgery can reliably occur. Look anywhere,

and you will see that nature's open grain is receptive to providential intervention—God's and ours. Even as God can be known through providential moments of concurrence, God can be known through the accessible nature of reality.

Theologian Abraham Kuyper believed every component of the universe was a thought in the mind of God before it ever came to be.[17] All that exists was purposeful. In its way, the physical universe images a God who is open to the agency of others. When Abraham and Moses entreated God to change direction, God did.[18] Even as God receives our adulation, God also receives our hypotheses and awe at the glory of the cosmos. We can trust that God's heart is receptive to us when the universe receives science's interventions. We can know something of God's mind through the *nature* of nature in this regard.

God can be known through the accessible nature of reality.

KNOWING GOD THROUGH PROVIDENTIAL INTERVENTION

God made *concurrence* and an *accessible universe* to fit together so we could know God more fully.

When our thinking syncs with the Creator's thinking, when a way of seeing fits with how nature is made to be seen, or when the timing of an action is right on time, it is as though the world is as it should be—we see things as they are.

To be a human being is to recognize this kind of fit. Our rational natures are made to fit with the rational nature of what we observe. We're made to see what is meant to be seen, at just the right time. Human beings are meant for the deep joy and contentment

of *shalom* (engaging the world as it should be). When those who do their intervening work in science discover how they fit into God's universe, they are more fully themselves. This is what God wants for them. When a scientific act syncs with a providentially accessible world, scientists are closer to God's intervening presence.

When science is close to God, we can all be closer to God.

> **Human beings are meant for the deep joy and contentment of shalom (engaging the world as it should be).**

LECTIO SCIENTIA

Increasing Your Providential Awareness

When it comes to God's providence, most of us have no idea what's going on.

There's a YouTube video that begins with the question, "How fast are you moving right now?"[19] The obvious answer is *not at all*—if you're stationary and reading these words. But then the narrator reframes the question, "But what about relative to the rest of the universe?" The clip goes on to describe just how fast we really *are* moving. If you live at the equator, you're spinning around the earth's axis at 1040 mph. As this is happening, the earth is orbiting the sun at 66,667 mph. As that is happening, the sun is moving toward other stars at 43,000 mph, even as it's moving upward—relative to the Milky Way plane—at 15,000 mph. "In addition to all of that, the Sun orbits the center of the Milky Way . . . moving at 483,000 mph . . . [meaning] we're moving at about 540,000 mph as a Solar System."[20] Of course, the Milky Way is also moving through the universe—at approximately 1,300,000 mph. Altogether, you're moving

through the universe at a combined speed of 1,900,000 mph!

This cosmic journey is evidence of only a small part of God's universe-keeping power. John Calvin wrote, "Unless the Spirit of the Lord upholds *everything*, it all lapses back into nothingness."[21] God sustains every law of nature that enables everything that fills the universe to exist—and even all of that is nothing compared to the incomprehensible nature of the being of God.

Thankfulness makes us receptive, and receptivity invites intimacy, revealing a God who is close and knowable.

It's this God who holds all things together in and through Christ.

Again, for the most part, we have no idea. While it's obvious that a human being can never fully grasp the scope and magnitude of God's providential work, we do get glimpses. Often these glimpses are born out of gratitude. When we are thankful for all that works in our world, we're closer to our gift-giving God. Thankfulness makes us receptive, and receptivity invites intimacy, revealing a God who is close and knowable.

PRACTICE

What if you try to connect the next scientific truth you encounter to an attribute of our ever-near God? If everything comes from God's mind, then everything has something to say about God's nature. Take gravity for instance. Thank God for this universal law that keeps everything in place in relation to everything else. God sets your feet on solid ground, He is a sure foundation, and He is the ultimate gravitational force—drawing in all things. God's gravitational nature can be contemplated with every step you take.

Of course, you can't think about this stuff all the time. You wouldn't have time for anything else! But you can think about it

more. The same Spirit who holds the universe in place holds you in place and knows the right time for all things.

Adjust your plans to make time to read your Bible more. Engaging God's nature through the Scriptures will give you more with which to recognize God's nature in creation.

Prayerfully consider these words and let them shape your perceptions: "For in him all things were created: things in heaven and on earth, visible and invisible, whether thrones or powers or rulers or authorities; all things have been created through him and for him. He is before all things, and in him all things hold together" (Col. 1:16–17).

PRAY

Heavenly Father, we have no idea how much You hold everything in every way. Help us see what can never be fully seen. Help us know how much You move. Give us a deeper understanding of the immensity of Your cosmos-keeping providence. May the held-ness of all things help us know how much we are held.

CHAPTER FOUR

SENSING GOD'S PRESENCE
VIA A GIANT SQUID

A Word from Matthew Morris

WHEN I ENTERED the marine biology program at Dalhousie University in Halifax, Nova Scotia, I learned there was a world of difference between reading about the ocean and experiencing the ocean. The sounds, smells, textures, and, yes, tastes of the ocean are not things that can be adequately described. They must be experienced to be understood.

I did not fully appreciate the role my senses played in my ability to worship God until I experienced the creatures of the ocean. In my invertebrate zoology class, my instructor handed me a living sand dollar. You have likely seen these creatures before—a bleached white shell with a delicate star etched into its disc-shaped body. When I was a kid, you could buy these creatures, dried and skeletal, as an image of Christ—five holes in the disc represented the pierced hands, feet, and side of Jesus, the central "Easter lily" and "nativity star." If you broke its body open, out would pour five "doves" (small bones that constitute the jaw of the creature) that represented goodwill and peace. As powerful as that imagery may be, I was not prepared for the actuality of the living creature.

For starters, the sand dollar wasn't white at all. It was a rich brown on all sides. And it didn't feel skeletal; its hardness was tempered by a velvety soft coating. It could crawl. It could bury itself in the sand. Here in my hand was a creature who lived by the rhythms of the ocean depths, within whose veins ran not blood but salt water to operate a strange series of bulbs and tube feet. The sand dollar knew nothing of forward or backward. With its mouth on its underside, it encountered all directions head-on. The creature had no visible eyes, no visible legs, no visible sense organs of any kind; and yet it could sense me. It could retreat if it felt threatened. I had to be gentle.

My professor encouraged me to view the sand dollar under the microscope. What I saw cannot be adequately replicated in words; indeed, for some of you this might sound absolutely disgusting. The entire surface of the creature was covered in microscopic tentacles, the cause of its velvety texture. Each little clear tube moved independently of the other, and their movements did not appear random. Over in this corner, the tentacles were moving debris off the sand dollar's body. Over here they were guiding food to its oral surface. Down here they seemed to be sensing the side of the petri dish. This was a creature of intelligence. I can barely conduct one task with my four limbs; imagine coordinating different activities among thousands of limbs! All at once I felt the transcendent nature of this being and by extension the sheer transcendence of its Creator. My senses had awakened to the reality of a creature that pointed beyond itself—not through some pithy symbolism but through the very nature of its embodied being. I knew then and there that God loves bodies, including my own.

It became clear to me that creatures are not facts to be compiled. They are their own worlds, vast mysteries that image the mystery of their Creator. Genetics, epigenetics, metabolomics, systems biology, developmental biology, microbiomics, ecology—each reveals new surprises about sand dollar biology that were already known by God, and each opens up research avenues that cannot, I believe, ever be exhausted.

I have since had other such encounters with God's good creation. I try to shape my undergraduate biology labs in a way that gives students the opportunity to encounter God as I did.

In this chapter, you will learn ways in which our senses work with science to bring us into a deeper understanding of God.

Dr. Matthew Morris is a devoted Christian, husband, father of three, and fish enthusiast. He is associate professor of biology at Ambrose University in Calgary, Alberta.

4

SENSING GOD'S PRESENCE VIA A GIANT SQUID

"Am I not present everywhere,
whether seen or unseen?"

JEREMIAH 23:24 MSG

In 2013, Dr. Tsunemi Kubodera, a zoologist with the Japanese National Museum of Nature and Science, sighted what he had been seeking his entire life—a living giant squid, a type of squid that had never been photographed or filmed alive. Its image was the "most elusive . . . in natural history."[1] "We know nothing about where or how it lives," said Kubodera before the find. "[It's] a gigantic creature, shrouded in mystery, but that's the attraction for me."[2]

With the help of several scientists, Dr. Kubodera finally found what he was searching for. With childlike elation, the team crowded around the video monitor to view the giant squid take the offered bait. For Dr. Kubodera, however, just seeing the giant squid through the video feed (from an unmanned probe) wasn't enough. "I just want to watch [the] Giant Squid [with] my eyes," he said.[3] His words

reminded me of the words of Job in the Old Testament: "I will see [God] for myself. Yes, I will see him with my own eyes. I am overwhelmed at the thought!" (Job 19:27 NLT).

For Dr. Kubodera, that day came when, with just the right submersible technology, at just the right depth, with just the right bait and bioluminescent light, at just the right time, he and his team saw with their own eyes what had never been seen before—this beautiful, powerful predator with its ten-inch diameter eyes and graceful tentacles, lunging onto the bait. When the bright submersible lights came on, the giant squid lingered as though posing for its debut. It was a holy moment. "That's incredible," gasped Kubodera. "What a surprise! It really, really came. It's shining like gold. Oh wow! Look at how that body shines. Look! Look at that eye!"[4] (The giant squid has the largest eyes on the planet.)

After a forty-year search, Dr. Kubodera saw what he had, perhaps, been created to see; a mystery was made clear. His sense of sight (aided by a submersible's lights, sustained by the deep-sea life support systems, and focused steadfastly for two hours) finally engaged a giant squid, this mysterious sea creature that uniquely reflected its mysterious Maker.

The God of all mystery created the giant squid—with its magnificent eyes and unknown paths. God made a creature that could see and go where most others could not. Even the ocean depths are not dark to the giant squid! For eons, this ever-elusive creature has been living and moving in unseen ways.[5] Its very existence is a pointer to the ways of God. "Your way was through the sea, your path through the great waters; yet your footprints were unseen" (Ps. 77:19 ESV). Even though God's ways are beyond our ways—and often beyond our ability to perceive them—God is still very much present and on the move. In a profound sense, the ways of the giant squid echo the ways of its Maker. The ways of Dr. Kubodera in his scientific passion

to unveil creation's mysteries also carry an echo of humanity's greater passion to know God.

Even as Dr. Kubodera was "made" for that moment when he would see what he was searching for, we are made to see God. What if God embedded a piece of the mystery of the divine nature into the giant squid's nature so that when human beings finally felt the elation of seeing a giant squid, we would have a foretaste of the elation of one day seeing God? The story of *Tsunemi Kubodera and the Giant Squid* is a parable in this regard. The kingdom of God is like a man who spent his whole life searching for a squid of great mystery.

> **God embedded a piece of the mystery of the divine nature into the giant squid's nature.**

Every human has an implanted *sense of God*—something deep inside that compels us to seek out and uncover the Mystery.[6] Like Dr. Kubodera, his team, and other scientists, we have all been given a collection of senses that enable us to engage unseen things. God has put sensing capacities into human beings that compel and enable us to see God![7] These capacities to reach for God fit with what we are designed by God to reach for. Even as a scientist's empirical sensibilities and technologies can be just right for seeing a giant squid, our innate sense of God is just right for seeing God.

When we see God, we will be like a persevering Japanese zoologist who finally sees a giant squid face to face, and we will exclaim:

> How many are your works, LORD!
>   In wisdom you made them all;
>   the earth is full of your creatures.
> There is the sea, vast and spacious,
>   teeming with creatures beyond number—
>   living things both large and small. **PS. 104:24-25**

And we can add our own admiration to the actual words found in Scripture:

The giant squid in its mysterious glory,
its paths untraceable, and vision so deep.
How many are your works, Lord!
May all creation glorify your Holy Name.

Job understood the revelatory nature of creation:

"But ask the animals, and they will teach you,
or the birds in the sky, and they will tell you;
or speak to the earth, and it will teach you,
or let the fish in the sea inform you.
Which of all these does not know
that the hand of the LORD has done this?
In his hand is the life of every creature
and the breath of all mankind." **JOB 12:7-10**

When God created the world, humankind was given a calling: "Be fruitful and increase in number; fill the earth and subdue it" (Gen. 1:28). In response to this command, one of the things humanity pursued was science. To the giant squid God said, "Be fruitful and increase in number and fill the water in the seas" (Gen. 1:22), and the giant squid, in its graceful, predatory, ever-elusive way, obeyed and produced millions of offspring.

The book of Revelation says: "Then I heard *every* creature in heaven and on

> **This is why we have eyes and why we have science: God wants us to see. To be human is to sense God through all that has been made.**

earth and under the earth and *on the sea, and all that is in them,* saying: 'To him who sits on the throne and to the Lamb be praise and honor and glory and power, for ever and ever!'" (Rev. 5:13, emphasis mine).

All the creatures that live in the sea are going to say these words. Millions of giant squid are going to offer their golden, shimmering praise. This is God's plan for this amazing sea creature. If a giant squid is seen and valued by God, then surely we need to see the giant squid for what it is—to catch a glimpse of our Creator in what He has made.

This is why we have eyes and why we have science: God wants us to see. To be human is to sense God through all that has been made: "My ears had heard of you but now my eyes have seen you" (Job 42:5).

SCIENCE AND THE SENSES

According to philosopher John Locke, "There is nothing in the intellect that was not earlier in the senses."[8] In order to know God through creation, God gave us the capacity to sense. Our bodies can touch, see, hear, smell, and taste the world around us. Technology has amplified these senses. Now we can touch the surface of Mars, see into our DNA, hear gravitational waves, smell diseases, and digitally unpack our taste buds. Through the advances of science and technology, we can sense what used to be imperceptible, what had previously moved too fast, too slow, invisibly, too far away, or too long ago.

This increased sensory perception has allowed humanity to interact at a deeper level with the nature of the universe, and each sense helps us engage material reality in a unique way.

The sense of touch concretizes our awareness of place. When we touch something, we know where we are. We know our place in relation to what we're touching. Touching increases our awareness of physical and temporal presence. As our sense of presence increases, we have more information with which to engage the shape, texture, and temperature of the object we are touching. From a faith perspective, the more present we are to our place, the closer we are to knowing God's presence in that place. From a scientific perspective, whenever technology touches something we've never touched before, humanity has a better sense of its place in the universe. When humanity knows where it is, it has more with which to know where God is. The better science is at touching things, the better we'll know where we are and the better we'll know the God who is reaching out to us everywhere because He is present in every part of His creation.

The sense of sight looks deeply, broadly, and far away. With sufficient light, our eyes can see numerous things at various depths in multiple directions, all at the same time. While the sense of touch excels up close, seeing has range. This range enables us to judge distance, perceive color, and discern patterns. Through sight—aided by an electron microscope—we can see the neural connections that make up a fruit fly's brain. Peering through the James Webb Space Telescope, we witness a deep field of galaxies light-years away. With technology's help, sight can engage both imperceptibly small and unimaginably large things. A human being can hold a photo of a fruit fly's brain in one hand and a photo of a field of galaxies in the other. This kind of range points us to an all-seeing God. Although the distant reaches of what science sees is often presented through grainy, photo-enhanced images, God sees all things clearly. Whenever science sees *more* it becomes an icon of an all-seeing God.

Hearing is an omni-perceptive sense. Right now, you can concurrently hear dozens of different sounds. Many of those sounds are

coming from sources you cannot touch or see. Hearing can happen through walls and, with the right technology, over great distances. When Caltech's David Reitze, executive director of the Laser Interferometer Gravitational-Wave Observatory (LIGO), announced that scientific history had been made—that for the first time humanity heard what Albert Einstein hypothesized a hundred years earlier—Reitze said, "We did it! . . . Up until now we've been deaf [to gravitational waves] . . . but now we are able to hear them."[9] Humanity could hear the sound that a ripple in the fabric of space-time made when two black holes collided eons ago. Even as those scientists were hearing gravitational waves for the first time, they were hearing each other breathe, gasp in astonishment, and cheer in response.[10] And God was hearing it all.

> **Whenever science sees more *it becomes an icon of an all-seeing God.***

Smell sees around corners. It knows what's going on even if it can't touch, see, or hear what's happening. Smell alerts us to the unseen—a freshly baked loaf of bread, rotting garbage, or a blooming garden. In the ancient church, perfumes were a "marker of divine presence, signifying the condition of blessing or grace."[11] Theophrastus, a third-century BC Greek philosopher, wrote that everything has its own distinctive smell that conveys not only identity, but also condition and circumstance.[12] Smell also enables time travel. The scent of lavender can take you back to a time when you were a child in your grandmother's garden. Dogs can smell lingering odors that were present twenty minutes before they arrived. The sense of smell reminds us that God is present everywhere, knowing all the details of our identity, condition, and circumstance.

Like smell, the sense of taste is connected to our emotions and memories. Good tastes comfort and enliven us while bad tastes repel and unsettle us. Taste is processed in the same part of our brains as

memories, and perhaps Jesus considered that when He asked His followers to remember Him through a communion meal. Taste differs from the other senses through its connection to bodily sustenance. The sense of taste inspires us to eat, keeps us eating, and protects us from things we shouldn't eat. By giving us a sense that brings joy to physiological necessity, God ensures our physical well-being. By keeping us healthy, God sustains us and all our senses.

God has given us an amazing range of senses and has exponentially increased their capacities through science and technology so we can more fully engage the physical universe. God makes more of our senses and knows that the more we sense and understand how things work, the more we'll sense and understand our Maker.

To more fully reveal Himself, God created a universe that can be sensed, made human beings with the bodily senses needed to engage creation, and then took on a human body with human senses in the person of Jesus. Through Jesus, God blessed and gave an imprimatur to our senses, showing us what they were made for: "Look at the birds of the air . . . listen and understand . . . take, eat . . . touch me and see."[13]

Through Christ, creation becomes a theater of God's glory. And through Christ (via the cosmos-sensing work of physicists, chemists, biologists, physicians, researchers, and all who work in science-related fields), humanity can know God more.

SENSING THE SENSE-ABLE

Through the senses, science engages a sense-able world.

God is present at both ends of this sense and sense-ability equation. God made our senses, and science collectively images a God who touches, sees, hears, smells, and tastes (metaphorically in

relation to a God who has no body, and literally through Christ). God created a sense-able world, one that is knowable through our senses. When humanity is more attentive to God's presence on both ends of this equation, we increase our capacity to experience God in the sensing moment.

It has often been said that attentiveness starts with gratitude. For the God-seeker, gratitude begins with acknowledging that God gave us the gift of our senses and the sense-able world, which brings God near. As we step into a sensing moment, our awareness of reality increases. Even as our senses register what we're sensing, we are relating to God: in seeing we are seen, in hearing we are heard, in understanding we are understood. As the sensory engagement process deepens, so too can our awareness of God's presence.

Relating to God in a sensing moment does not always play out automatically or perfectly. Our senses and technologies are limited. The things we're trying to sense are complex and elusive. When we come

> **For the God-seeker, gratitude begins with acknowledging that God gave us the gift of our senses.**

to know one truth, a whole new set of unknowns unfolds. These limitations are humbling, but God can use this humility. The smaller we get, the less we're in the way. Good science requires objectivity. We need to follow the data and not read what we think we know into the facts.

Humility is a crucial spiritual-sensing catalyst. To know God is to know our limits. We are called to submit to and follow the Maker of all data. The more we submit, the more we see—the less it's about us, the more it's about God. In this place, an epiphany can occur, and the observer can become the observed. Even as scientists sense the world, they can realize that God is sensing them. The God

who sees and knows everything sees and knows us. God wants us to know—and to be known.

God came to this world through Christ so we could know God more. Jesus took on human senses and engaged a sensible world so that He could share with us what He knows. More than anyone, Jesus could sense and perceive God's Word through nature and human nature. All things were made through Him, and now, seated at the right hand of God, He knows all of creation's secrets. Because we know Him, we can know some of those secrets too.

> **To know God is to know our limits. We are called to submit to and follow the Maker of all data.**

To truly sense reality is to be in a place where *Christ in you* senses *Christ in creation*. It all comes together in Christ. To know Him in your soul is to know Him in creation. With Spirit-renewed senses, we can see Jesus more clearly in creation. We can be as present to Him (via creation) as His disciples were when they were seeing, hearing, and walking right beside Him.

LECTIO SCIENTIA

Waking Your Senses

If matter matters to God, then it ought to matter to us.

One way to realize that matter matters is to sense it more fully—with all our beings, so that we can better sense God's being. Augustine said, "I can experience far more than I can understand about the Trinity."[14] There's a sense-based knowing that transcends words. While our senses alone can never get us to God, they can bring us closer.

So the question becomes: Is there a way to sharpen our senses so we can more fully engage God's matter-loving heart?

In Psalms 38 and 51, David prays with his lips, mouth, tongue, intestines, muscles, bones, skin, thighs, heart, lungs, eyes, ears, and throat.[15] It's this kind of whole-bodied engagement that enables a more sense-able engagement of God through science. This is how God made us. We're not just rational beings; we're embodied, multisensory beings. When things go off the rails, we feel sick to our stomachs. When we're in danger or in love, our hearts race. We are stilled when confronted with beauty. The Christian faith is a whole-bodied faith. According to the Bible, to know something is not merely a rational exercise. To really know is to live out what you know with all your physical being.

According to theologian Belden Lane, "Knowing the full range of sensory experience [is] . . . a measure of one's creaturehood before God."[16] The more you engage the world through your senses, the more you experience yourself as a creature who

> **The Christian faith is a whole-bodied faith.**

is part of something bigger. You realize you are not alone in this world. Increased sensory awareness affirms that you're a small part of a larger whole. This sense-driven humility evokes a before-the-face-of-God humility. A sense-able awareness of your surroundings leads to a clearer sense of the God who surrounds you. To feel like a creature is your most natural state of being. When faced with your Creator, how can you feel like anything but a creature?

Engaging the world—with all of our God-designed senses—leads us to this sense of creaturehood. Even as the trees respond to God in a tree-like way and ants in an ant-like way, we are called to engage God in human-like ways. In Psalm 63 David prays, "You, God, are my God, earnestly I seek you; I thirst for you, my *whole being* longs

for you" (v. 1). David knew that he was made to know God through *all* that he was.

PRACTICE

When scientists engage one of God's creatures—a molecule, a planet, an animal, or an element of an ecosystem—they are imaging their Creator. With each touch, they nudge us toward the God who touched us through Christ. With every observation, they point to an ever-observant God. When they listen to God's creatures, they model the ever-listening presence of the Holy Spirit. When science senses creation, it affirms God's presence through its sensory image-bearing.

Imagine how your sense of God's nearness would change if you interpreted science experiments, observations, or discoveries in this light. Keep this sense of God's nearness through His creation in mind as you engage the discoveries that fill our science-filled world.

When a new discovery catches your attention, ask,

- How does this specific scientific method or technology reflect the sensing nature of God?

- How do the scientists and technologists—in wielding this scientific method or technology—image the sensing nature of God?

Write down any Scripture passages or theological truths that come to mind as you engage these questions. Bring God's sensing truth in the Scriptures into conversation with God's sensing truth in the science. Let them co-illuminate one another.

As science contributes to the whole picture of a world-sensing God, let your sense of creatureliness grow. Let science humble you

and show you your place. Be reminded of the fact that, even as everything that surrounds you is made, you are made.

PRAY

Almighty God, Maker of heaven and earth, quicken my senses. Help me see, hear, taste, smell, and feel Your presence more. You made my senses; help me fully *be* in this body of mine—in this body of Yours. As You surround me with a universe filled with creatures, re-create me and renew my sense of You.

CHAPTER FIVE

TREE BRANCHES, WOUND HEALING, AND AN INTERDEPENDENT GOD

A Word from Vern Peters

AS I READ GOD SPEAKS SCIENCE, I am reminded of several conversations with colleagues at the Christian university, where I teach. The first conversation occurred, when I interviewed for a position as a forest ecologist. I was asked, "What are the great books you have read? How have you come to your convictions to integrate your faith with your discipline?" I paused to think how my training as an ecologist, where studying tree growth and forest development after fire was relevant to the mission of a Christian university, and the role of the church in society.

My answer was embarrassingly simple. "I do science (forest ecology), and I've spent a lot time in nature, thinking, and studying God's creation, and I think other people should know these things too". How could "one book," the creation, testify to a panel of theologians, philosophers, historians, in addition to scientists? I think what they heard in my answer, was that I study the book of creation. While I might use different approaches than them, I, like them, studied the book of creation. I just studied the chapter that ecology reveals. My colleagues saw the

91

congruence of this chapter with the chapters of philosophy, theology, and art, and knew that these chapters collectively spoke the language of God.

Another conversation occurs every year in my opening lecture to an introductory biology class, that studies the diversity of life. I often ask a question that surprises students. "How do we know God?" I remind them that we know God by His spoken word, and by His works in creation (Rom. 1:20). This "two books" approach is a historical view on the manner of God's self-revelation, and was endorsed by church fathers in the Westminster Confession of the sixteenth century. So much for novelty, as a twenty-first-century Christian that happens to be a scientist!

Old approaches work. I now sometimes teach with parables when I'm trying to help students see the relevance of science to their daily lives and faith. Christ used this approach too John's coverage of our conversation on tree branches, provides an example of this. I'll provide another—in John 15:1–4, Christ identifies Himself as the true vine for bearing fruit in our lives. This metaphor is instructive if we let our minds turn to plant and fungal relationships. Mutualistic fungi called mycorrhizae not only increase the absorptive area of plant root hairs a hundredfold, but facilitate the exchange of water and nutrients, for plant sugars. They surround individual cells of their host, even penetrate them, accelerating the exchange of their commodities. "If a man remains in me, and I remain in him, he will bear much fruit." The plant fungal relationship casts fresh light on how interwoven this dependence might be.

When God speaks science, I think He is doing it through parables, or metaphors. As scientists, we can see half of the

metaphor in an empirical way, but we need a storyteller to give it meaning. God's narrative of the creation is a grand story laid out for us to read. Reading this story in a manner where our understanding of scientific processes affords new understanding of God's self-revelation is the invitation given to humanity.

Dr. Vernon Peters, Professor of Ecology, The King's University, and Professor of Conservation Biology, The Au Sable Institute of Environmental Studies.

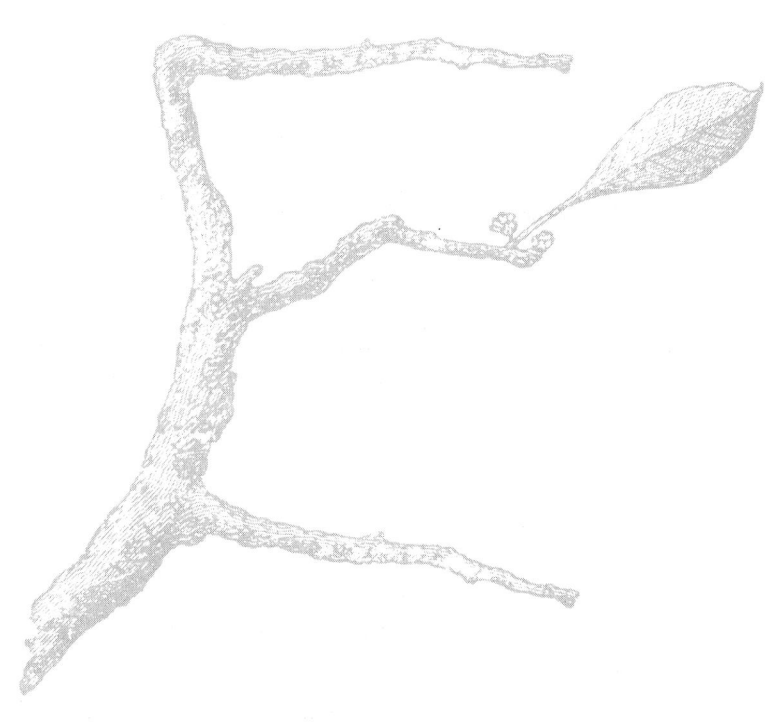

TREE BRANCHES, WOUND HEALING, AND AN INTERDEPENDENT GOD

"I am the true vine, and my Father is the gardener.
He cuts off every branch in me that bears no fruit, while every
branch that does bear fruit he prunes so that it will be even more
fruitful. . . . Remain in me, as I also remain in you.
No branch can bear fruit by itself; it must remain in the vine.
Neither can you bear fruit unless you remain in me."

JOHN 15:1-4

Several years ago, I contacted a biology professor for some spiritual direction. I was studying Jesus' teaching on the vine and the branches and needed some plant-science help.

I wanted to know—from a biological perspective—how branches "remain" in their vines. I thought a better understanding of the science of remaining could deepen my understanding of the biblical metaphor of remaining, so I asked Dr. Vern Peters from The King's

University in Edmonton what makes a branch/trunk connection ideal for a tree's flourishing.

Apparently, there *is* no ideal when it comes to plant science.

It's always a compromise, between better and worse. . . . It all depends on the pressures any particular tree faces. Some trees require rapid growth with high branch turnover, while some need to grow tall and sacrifice lower branches more quickly to grow tall. Some need lateral growth to acquire light, and that impacts branching. Some are not as strong a competitor but tolerate the little remaining resources by growing slowly and, in so doing, expand their lifespans. Some need more radial growth to strengthen the trunk. . . . We never look at an organism and see it as perfectly adapted. . . . What's fascinating is that even in the lifetime of a single tree, that single tree will often modify its growth form as a reflection of the environmental conditions it experiences. So, there isn't even one ideal form for a single plant. Plants are highly flexible and highly responsive to their environment and really only grow to the extent that a particular environment allows them to.[1]

Dr. Peters went on to apply this plant-science wisdom to the life of a follower of Christ:

When I look at plants and think about how Christians respond to the pressures of their environment, they may be inclined to say, "Well, this is how God has made me." But there is also a tremendous capacity for God to work and transform and mold us to be servants in different settings. We need to be responsive to that. We need to recognize our gifting and our calling and serve where we are perhaps most effective. Within that too, there's incredible capacity for growth.[2]

Dr. Peters's spiritual insight was both freeing and humbling. There may be as many ways to remain in Jesus as there are differing branch configurations in response to ever-varying environmental conditions. This can be incredibly freeing for people of faith who struggle with the constraints of thinking there is only one way to respond to God. As they remain in Jesus, people with every kind of personality in every kind of circumstance respond to God in wonderfully varied and faithful ways.

> **When it comes to engaging a universe conceived by a communal God (Father, Son, and Holy Spirit), working in community is a vital tool.**

To believe that there is only one ideal way for a branch to function is unrealistic and limiting. Yet that's what I (implicitly) used to believe as a spiritual leader.

A plant scientist corrected my theology.

By submitting my metaphorical reading of the scriptural text to a plant scientist's empirical understanding of branches, a richer interpretation of Jesus' teaching resulted. Science enriched my theology. This is what can happen when differing disciplines engage one another. When you look at something through a different lens, you see things differently. This, of course, is the value of any communal engagement. Together we have more resources to help us discern reality.

When it comes to engaging a universe conceived by a communal God (Father, Son, and Holy Spirit), working in community is a vital tool.

A COMMUNAL GOD

God is relational. The triune God is an interdependent community of life, joy, wisdom, power, grace, and love. Each person of the Trinity

has a unique nature and role, and yet the three are one. They relate to one another in mutually submissive, cooperative, symbiotic, and synergistic ways. The Father loves the Son, the Son glorifies the Father, and the Spirit proceeds from the Father and Son. Jesus does everything in accordance with the will of the Father and perfectly images, embodies, and exemplifies the Father's nature. All that Jesus does fits with who the Father is. The Spirit speaks what it hears from Jesus and the Father, and all that the Spirit does points back to them. The Father is the wellspring of all things. He creates, sustains, sends, directs, and gives life to everything.

All that God made reflects God's relationality.

The universe was made by this triune God. Everything in the cosmos was created for relationship. All that God made reflects God's relationality. All things are interdependent.

We see this interdependent relationality in tree branches, but we can also see it in the graceful dance of electrons, protons, and neutrons in the atom and in the chemical bonds that make up molecules. For example, a cascade of enzymes are repairing trillions of DNA breaks per second in your body, the white blood cells of your immune system are actively pursuing pathogens, and your immune system is perpetually interacting with your body's cardiovascular, musculoskeletal, endocrine, exocrine, digestive, nervous, renal, and respiratory systems. The relational nature of reality is evident in how your body moves in concert with all the other bodies on this planet and in the co-mingling of our world's social, political, economic, and ecological systems. The relational nature of reality is demonstrated by the gravitational pull of our solar system and in our careening galaxy's place among the two hundred billion galaxies in the universe.

Everything is interconnected and relational—including science.

Science's methodology is relational. New discoveries are built on the findings of earlier theories. Researchers from around the world work together to seek out a cure. Through rigorous teaching, writing, peer review, mentoring, and methodological systems, science grows in community. Science interdependently interacts with the physical reality it engages. It listens to and follows the data. Science takes its cues from what nature presents and depends on what nature reveals. Nobody sees the whole picture. Everyone works on their own puzzle piece; there is no one leader, agenda, or plan.[3] Science operates with a collective intelligence—like how bees and ants work. While individuals hypothesize, develop theories, experiment, and plan next steps, they are ultimately led by a greater truth—the data.

> **God wants to be more fully known. The Spirit that hovered over the waters at creation hovers over scientific imaginations today.**

Data guides science and is its relational language. It enables science to communally engage a relational universe that was created by a relationally interdependent God.

Science models what it's like to follow God by the way it follows the physical data. To get to the truth, you need to put your personal agenda aside and submit to a greater truth. By working in community, science reflects the nature of a communal God.

It takes a community to engage what was communally made. We need the fullness of physics, biology, and chemistry to even begin to understand the fullness of a theology of Father, Son, and Holy Spirit. We need the wisdom of every academic discipline.

God wants to be more fully known. The Spirit that hovered over the waters at creation hovers over scientific imaginations today. In a deeply mysterious and communal way, the Spirit orients our imaginations toward a universe-conceiving God.

INTERDEPENDENCE IN WOUND HEALING

While at a conference a few years ago, I met a molecular biologist who had just made an amazing discovery. Dr. Cymbeline Culiat had identified the functions of a unique signaling protein that could lead to therapies to improve wound healing. She was the first human being to demonstrate that this protein was important in soft tissue formation and could be developed into treatments for hard-to-heal injuries (such as wounds in diabetic patients).

When I asked Dr. Culiat what the nature of that signaling protein might teach us about the nature of God, she responded in general terms by talking about the protein's role in cell maturation and death and the communal nature of wound healing within the body as a whole. I pushed further, asking what the *unique* nature of the protein reveals about the *unique* nature of God. Dr. Culiat detailed how this protein helps produce the right environment for healing to occur. Her description reminded me how God moves in intricate, complex, and mysterious ways to produce the right context for any healing that occurs in life. The Holy Spirit creates, guides, and preserves every detail in such a way that we, and everything that fills the cosmos, can fully mature and be restored when wounded.

Dr. Culiat told me that this new way of engaging God through her work was transformative for her, expressing gratitude for how the communal healing work of science and the communal healing mechanisms of the body connect to the communal healing heart of God:

> I have now become deliberate or intentional in viewing my work and am thinking deeply about how it illustrates not only biological but also spiritual truths. I've grown beyond the usual, "Oh, it's so beautiful or that's an impressive complex phenomenon/biological process/structure, therefore I worship

and thank God" to discerning how [new data] illustrates the *nature* of God and his purpose. What does my work tell me about his nature and his purpose for me and us and this world? This perspective has become deeply ingrained and integrated in my work.[4]

God wants to be deeply ingrained and integrated into our lives and work, and the context for this integration is interdependence, *remaining* in Christ.

When a scientific community discovers, names, and stewards a regenerative protein, we can see evidence of a God who works both with and within us to heal.

When we recognize God's interdependent handiwork in a newly discovered biological pathway and acknowledge that the recognition came through the communal efforts of science, we realize that both protein and science belong to God, and we are drawn into a deeper relationship with our Maker.

Right now, deep inside each of our bodies, unseen healing is playing out. Before we even have the tools to consider God's role in this, we are already being restored. There's a built-in goodness God has infused into creation. We can know and experience God as we interdependently engage this goodness.

INTERDEPENDENT INDWELLING

God operates in interdependent ways—ways that help us know and experience Him. Sometimes this happens through His nudging our expectations in a new direction, as He did with the molecular biologist Dr. Culiat.

To notice and engage God's interdependent presence, it helps to

increase awareness of the dependencies at play in any given relational exchange.

Where *providential intervention* (chapter 3) focuses on the act of intervening (concurrence and accessibility) and *sensing the sense-able* (chapter 4) focuses on points of contact (sight, hearing, touch), *interdependent indwelling* focuses on the nature and direction of the dependencies at play during an interrelating act.

Interdependent relationships are always give-and-take; at times you are dependent and other times you are depended upon (and often both happen at the same time). This interweaving of dependencies makes relationships strong. We need others, and they need us. We all have something to give, and we are created to give what we have to others.

This reality plays out in ecological mutualisms known as an obligatory symbiosis—where two species benefit from and often become completely dependent on each other. Lichen is a good plant-science example of this kind of relationship. Here, two different kingdoms of biological organisms, algae and fungi (scientifically, about as far apart as two organisms can be) "come together to form one living association of organisms. Algae photosynthesize and provide 'food' to the fungi, while the fungi coat the algae with a protective layer of hyphal strands, preventing it from drying out and allowing it to live on land (all algae, by nature, are aquatic)."[5]

Jesus, of course, was God Himself, who doesn't *need* to depend on anything or anyone, but in the incarnation, Jesus took on a dependent role. Dr. Vern Peters sees Jesus' "dependence" on the church as a co-opting of labor similar to that of lichen: "God can intervene and accomplish His divine purposes apart from us but has chosen to involve us and allow us to contribute directly. We are given glimpses of His work being accomplished through our faithfulness (our choice to function as mutualists)."[6] In order to live on earth,

Jesus depended on a human body. God's work through Him was accomplished through Mary's faithful acceptance of the call to bear God's Son and through her willingness to nurse, care for, and protect a wholly dependent infant Jesus.

The connection Dr. Peters makes to the work of Jesus and the church can also be made to the work of science. God chooses to depend on and use science to help humanity understand and steward God's creational gifts. In a Christlike way, science is a means through which we can engage the truth. Science helps mediate creation's truth. When scientists, like branches, remain in relationship with their communities, they can bear God's scientific fruit and give us more resources to help us know God.

When scientists give every ounce of their cognitive capacity to the contemplation of a particular facet of nature, they image a God who put intense thought into all that is made. When a science student receives knowledge that has been accumulated over centuries through previous scientific discovery, it is like receiving God's grace—unmerited and something to be received with gratitude.

> **Science helps mediate creation's truth.**

Interdependent giving and receiving are essential for maximal flourishing.

In his book *The Lives of a Cell*, Dr. Lewis Thomas writes about the essential biological interdependencies that give us life. Our bodies, it seems, are not our own:

> We are shared, rented, occupied. At the interior of our cells, driving them, providing the oxidative energy that sends us out for the improvement of each shining day, are the mitochondria, and in a very strict sense they are not ours. . . . They are as

much symbionts as the rhizobial bacteria in the roots of beans. Without them we could not move a muscle, drum a finger, think a thought.

Mitochondria are stable and responsible lodgers and I choose to trust them . . . I like to think that they work in my interest, that each breath they draw [is] for me, but perhaps it is they who walk through the local park in the early morning, sensing my senses, listening to my music thinking my thoughts.[7]

Right now, these foreign bodies (the mitochondria) sustain our lives. What's striking about this interdependent relationship is that God put this system into play long ago. Before any of us came to be, God embedded the need for others into our physiologies. Our intrinsic dependence on mitochondria can point to our intrinsic dependence on both God and others. This dependence helps to make us more fully who we are.

DEPENDING ON GOD

To know God is the most essential thing for a person of faith. The ultimate gift you can give God is your whole life. The ultimate gift you can receive is God's life. To be united with God through Christ—a far deeper union than that of mitochondria and our cells—is to be alive in the greatest sense imaginable.

And the life God has for us is often unimaginable.

When German biophysics researcher Peter Hegemann uncovered how pond algae sense sunlight and regulate photosynthesis by moving up or down relative to the water's surface, he could never have imagined this discovery would lead to a technology that would

allow neurons to be turned on and off with light—enabling a deeper understanding of neural networks.[8] Algae have a protein that converts light into an electrical signal. Once a gene connected to this protein is inserted into a neuron, a photosensitive switch is created. Neuroscientists can now study the brain at a level previously unimagined—all because Peter Hegemann wanted to know what made pond algae go up and down.

This is the kind of surprise that can develop from communal interdependence, especially when the community is diverse. Right now, discoveries are being made in seemingly unrelated fields that will change the trajectory of science. To the extent that researchers graciously share what they've learned, read what others have learned, and apply these learnings back into their work—science grows. Through the give and take of diverse interdependence, humanity flourishes.

Even as the photosensitive workings of pond algae bring new light to the human brain, God brings light to us through an interdependent connection. Perhaps the best example of two disparate entities coming together is God and human beings! When they were brought together, the result was Jesus—humanity as it was intended to be.

Jesus is the key to understanding what interdependent indwelling can look like. The key to fruitful interdependence is remaining in Him. As we practice remaining in Christ, we'll grow toward becoming fully interdependent beings who are more humble, receptive, and giving—the way God made us to be.

Science gives us a front row seat to the vast interdependencies of the cosmos. The clarity science brings to the interdependencies of the universe is a gift to humanity and a pointer to Jesus, who invites us to remain in Him.

If humanity is made for God, then depending on God should be the most innate, natural, and life-giving thing imaginable for humanity.

Consider how the interdependencies of your body free you to grow.

Our smooth-muscle cells are born with complete instructions, in need of no help from us, and they work away on their own schedules, modulating the lumen of blood vessels, moving things through intestines, opening and closing tubules according to the requirements of the entire system. Secretory cells elaborate their products in privacy; the heart contracts and relaxes; hormones are sent off to react silently with cell membranes, switching adenyl cyclase, prostaglandin, and other signals on and off; cells communicate with each other by simply touching; organelles send messages to other organelles; all this goes on continually, without ever a personal word from us. The arrangement is that of an ecosystem, with the operation of each part being governed by the state and function of all the other parts. When things are going well, as they generally are, it is an infallible mechanism.[9]

Just as the interdependent power of our bodies enables us to get on with the higher-order activities of our daily lives, our interdependent place within God's body frees us to get on with our kingdom callings. Because God takes care of an infinite number of unseen, yet miraculous, processes in our bodies, we can freely ponder the meaning of life, think about God, write symphonies, and say prayers. Science works because God created and continues to hold a universe that is inter-dependable at all levels.

LECTIO SCIENTIA

Upping Your Relational Intelligence

Commenting on the thinking of Jonathan Edwards, historian George Marsden notes that "Everything is related because everything is related to God."[10] It's hard to read a sentence like that and *not* become more conscious of the weight of interdependence. If all things are related, then all that we do impacts others, even as all that they do impacts us. When we consider God's call to put others first—to do unto them as we would have them do unto us—the burden of interdependence grows. God calls us to extend love in a highly interconnected context. God knew this was the best context for holding divine love and allowing it to grow synergistically. For creation to fully contain the love of God, it needed to be this relationally connected (and receptive).

Interdependence, therefore, keeps our feet to the relational fire. Doing the wrong things, or not doing the right things, matters much more than we think. Good choices allow us to reflect God's image, bad choices diminish our capacity to experience God's presence.

John Calvin wrote, "Whenever we are encouraged to do damage or harm, let us remember that our Lord has provided lodging for us all in this world. . . . If I now seek to despoil the land of what God has given. . . . then I am seeking as much as I can to do away with God's goodness . . . Do I no longer want his grace to have currency and reign?"[11] Calvin goes on to write about damaging "trees and houses and similar things": "Our Lord ordained the land to be as it were our nursing mother, and when it opens its entrails to sustain us, we should know that this is just as if God extended his hand to us and handed us proofs of his goodness."[12]

In terms of our capacity to experience God's presence, when we act in interdependently ignorant ways, we diminish ourselves and we have fewer resources to help us relate to God's selfless interdependent presence. Instead of lovingly leaning into the world-flourishing power of interdependence, we work against it—sowing discord, disunity, and destruction. We need to let the interdependent weight of the cosmos lead us to act selflessly. When we help others in an interdependent system, we help ourselves. This kind of mutualism leads to intimacy—with others and with God.

> **When we help others in an interdependent system, we help ourselves. This kind of mutualism leads to intimacy—with others and with God.**

For Calvin, the end goal of our spiritual lives is union with Christ: "[We] put on Christ and are engrafted into his body," like a branch is engrafted into a vine.[13] We are united with the love of God through Christ. To know Christ's love fully is to know how He feels toward all He is related to—all that belongs to Him.

Science belongs to God—Father, Son, and Holy Spirit.

Whatever science unpacks and discovers is God's. God loves science and calls us to love it too. Even as God sustains us by way of the biological function of trees, the discoveries of insulin, giant magnetoresistance, and the human genome, God lovingly whispers to us through these life-enhancing scientific discoveries. God thinks about us through scientists who dream about making a better world. God protects us through their empirical environmental wisdom. When we lovingly support the sciences, attend to them, and engage in them, we're responding to all of God's loving, scientific gestures.

PRACTICE

To be united with Christ is to be in union with His physical creation. Science gives us the relational tools to do that. The next time you engage a scientific truth, treat the moment as though it was an introduction to a relative, a fellow creature of God's. Love what you're learning, listen well, and give it the respect it rightfully deserves. Attend to God's handiwork, and consider how you might support it and enable it to flourish.

The next time you encounter a creation-based metaphor in the Scriptures, do what I did at the beginning of this chapter—dig deeper into the science. Perhaps journal about how the deeper scientific understanding you've researched enriches your understanding of the biblical text.

PRAY

Lord, wake me to my interdependence. Help me see how my creaturely place in this world connects to my creaturely place before You. To know You is to know that all created things are related to You. To remain in You is to be one of many creatures doing the same. Let every branch remind me of this truth, I pray.

CHAPTER SIX

LANGUAGE ACQUISITION AND A MULTILINGUAL GOD

A Word from Ross Hastings

THE HUMAN CAPACITY to know is already a sign of grace and a source of wonder. This next chapter gives us a wonderful sense of this grace and wonder.

Our capacity to know gestures toward the existence of a revealing God who is also the Creator God who has endowed His image bearers with the givenness of the capacity to know. Together the revealing God and the receptive human speak of intelligibility. God has spoken in creation, and in person, and through Scripture, in ways that are intelligible, and we have the capacity (not without grace) to receive His knowledge in distinctive ways in each category.

In this chapter, you will discover that our human knowledge is personal. Interestingly, our knowledge of God, which is grounded in God's redemptive, regenerating grace, cannot be received apart from personal, experiential knowledge of God. Revelation is not just a knowledge category in Christian thought; it is a *communion* category. And that entails the whole Trinity—Father as revealer, Son as revealed, and Spirit as

revelation. Our knowing of God is intrinsically dependent upon the being of God.

The nature of our knowledge of God (epistemology) is very much dependent on the being of God (ontology). A particular illustration of this in theology is that the Son of God, who is also the eternal Word (*Logos*) of God, is the revealer of God through creation and through the redemption of humanity and creation. His ability to reveal God is dependent upon the fact that He is, and always has been, *God*. His ability to reveal God to humans is dependent upon the fact that He became *human*. Our knowing of God through the Word is dependent upon His being. What's more is that our pursuit of theological knowledge is grounded upon what was and what is. The task of theologians for centuries has been to offer imagination and thoughts and words that reflect as best they can, *a posteriori*, what transpired when God the Logos became flesh and lived among us. Our hope is that what we are describing bears a close resemblance to what really is. The theological task is humble.

The knowledge involved in science is equally humble. The hope is always that our epistemology reflects the ontology—that our knowledge of reality more closely mirrors that reality. Most thoughtful scientists profess to a humble way of knowing called critical realism, rather than logical positivism. That is, we assume that our knowing corresponds to the being of what is being studied and experimented with, and we conceive of our models in a way that best accounts for the evidence and data we have gained, always with an awareness that these may be modified. Chaos theory and quantum mechanics have tended to create this humble attitude.

This chapter will create within you a desire to know the Being described in science in order that you may know more richly the Being described in theology—and so restore a sense of awe, wonder and humility before the God of creation, revelation, and redemption.

W. Ross Hastings, PhD (chemistry, Queen's University, Ontario), PhD (theology, St. Andrews, Scotland), is Sangwoo Youtong Chee Professor of Theology, Regent College, and the author of Echoes of Coinherence: Trinitarian Theology and Science Together *(Cascade Press) and* The Resurrection of Jesus Christ: Exploring Its Theological Significance and Ongoing Relevance *(Baker Academic).*

LANGUAGE ACQUISITION AND A MULTILINGUAL GOD

Before a word is on my tongue you, LORD, know it completely.

PSALM 139:4

M IT researcher Deb Roy once gave a TED Talk called "The Birth of a Word,"[1] presenting his work on how young children learn language. To gather data, he installed audio and video recording devices throughout his home and captured ninety thousand hours of language development in his one-year-old son. Roy's fatherly delight at hearing his son learn the word *water* is contagious. At one point, Roy plays a forty-second time-lapse of six months of audio recordings that beautifully captures the transition from "gaaaa" to "water." When the toddler finally says the word *water* clearly, the audience spontaneously applauds.

Roy maps the data to analyze how the word *water* was born and uncovers a pattern in the child/caregiver feedback loop. Leading up to the birth of the word, caregiver utterances become shorter and shorter. Using ever-simpler language, the caregiver meets the child

en route to the place where the word is born. After the word is born, the utterances of both caregiver and child increase in length, enabling ongoing communication and, therefore, a relationship to grow.

Dr. Roy's findings remind me of God's words through the prophet Isaiah, "I have put my words in your mouth" (Isa. 51:16), and St. Augustine's observation that "how, indeed, would [God] be ready to be spent for [our] souls if he disdained to stoop to [our] ears?"[2] The parental act of simplifying words so they can be grasped is clearly a Godlike activity. Through the incarnation, God bent down and took on human language. Jesus conveyed the mysteries of God's kingdom through parables that a child could understand.

Stooping to our ears, the triune God (whose language is surely beyond our comprehension) puts scientific utterances like molecular structure, DNA repair mechanisms, and radiation physics into short, simple, and comprehendible phrases we can grasp. For centuries, God met science where it was at and taught it new words and enabled a relationship to grow. Like a good caregiver, God was delighted whenever we came to know something new—whenever we were able to say a new scientific word for the first time.

God teaches us new words so we can better know both God and the nature of the cosmos.

THE NEED TO KNOW

As humans, we long to know—to know the nature of things, to know how life works, and to know where we came from.

According to Nobel Prize–winning physicist Steven Weinberg, "The urge to trace the history of the universe back to its beginnings is irresistible."[3] It's irresistible because knowing where we came from helps us know both where and who we are. With every new bit of

knowledge, we become more ourselves. We understand and, like a child learning a new word, are both delighted and empowered.

Physicist and theologian John Polkinghorne writes, "The development of modern science has shown us that our human ability to understand the universe far exceeds anything that could reasonably be considered as simply . . . necessity, or a happy spinoff from necessity . . . our understanding of the workings of the world greatly exceeds anything that could simply be required for human survival."[4]

Maybe our capacity to know is disproportionate to what we need to know for mere human survival because we are created to know the fullness of God.

If we don't use our understanding for knowing God, it can fall short in problematic ways. C. S. Lewis notes,

> The books or the music in which we thought the beauty was located will betray us if we trust to them; it was not *in* them, it only came *through* them. . . . These things—the beauty, the memory of our own past—are good images of what we really desire; but if they are mistaken for the thing itself, they turn into dumb idols, breaking the hearts of their worshippers. For they are not the thing itself; they are only the scent of a flower we have not found, the echo of a tune we have not heard, news from a country we have never yet visited.[5]

Science's desire to know is a subset of a greater desire to know. The detection of gravitational waves is the echo of a tune. Our experience of olfactory senses is the scent of a flower. Reports of good scientific news come from a country we've never yet visited. The fact that science never gets to the end of things—either the infinite or the infinitesimal—points to how we're made for an even greater knowing: we're made to know God.

God knows that to be human is to possess knowledge and that we are most ourselves when we know Him. Human beings are made in the image of a God who knows everything. So to know how things work is to bear God's image more fully, and to bear God's image more fully is to know God more fully as well. The more science bears God's all-knowing image, the more we'll be able to know God through the creation-revealing work science does.

THE SENSUS DIVINITATIS

According to John Calvin, God planted the *need to know* into every human soul so that we would find God. Calvin called this the *sensus divinitatis*—a sense of the divine that causes human beings to yearn for and seek after God. This divine sense is so much a part of us that we cannot open our eyes without being compelled to see God.[6]

> *The fact that science never gets to the end of things points to how we're made for an even greater knowing: we're made to know God.*

One way God compels us to seek Him is through our need to know. Science engages the workings of the universe and can bring us closer to the Maker's understanding of the universe. This inner drive to empirically understand is connected to the need to spiritually understand. The need to know the nature of the cosmos is an integral part of our need to know God.

The kind of knowing conveyed in *sensus divinitatis* is different from empirical knowledge, however. A more mysterious kind of knowing, it's difficult to quantify and is distinct from rational observation. According to 2019 Templeton Prize winning physicist (and atheist) Marcelo Gleiser, the knowing we long for because of *sensus divinitatis* is more

spiritual and emotional: "When you find the solution or something that looks like a solution, you get emotionally moved to an amazing extent, especially when it's a surprising thing. You know, it really is a spiritual emotion . . . when I have this, it really is something transcendent."[7]

The 2017 Templeton Prize winning philosopher (and Christian), Alvin Plantinga, explains it this way:

> It isn't that one beholds the night sky, notes that it is grand, and concludes that there must be such a person as God: an argument like that would be ridiculously weak. It isn't that one notes some feature of the Australian outback—that it is ancient and brooding, for example—and draws the conclusion that God exists. It is rather that, upon the perception of the night sky or the mountain vista or the tiny flower, these beliefs just arise within us. They are *occasioned* by the circumstances; they are not conclusions from them.[8]

Sensus divinitatis-knowing wells up from within us; it comes from a place that is parallel to rational cognition.

When we experience this kind of knowing, the God who has embedded divine wisdom in creation pulls back the veil of what's empirically observable and reveals Himself. God causes something within us to recognize reality for what it is. God's presence in us (this *sensus divinitatis*) opens our eyes to God's presence through, in, behind, and before all things. God nudges and calls and transforms our need to empirically know into something more intimate and spiritual. Our satisfaction in simply knowing some*thing* becomes the greater satisfaction of knowing some*one*.

SCIENTIFIC KNOWING

Hungarian scientist Michael Polanyi long considered the nature of scientific knowing.[9] In his view, scientists can't make discoveries happen. Discoveries simply reveal what was previously unknown. Like coming to faith, they surprise us because they were beyond us. Theologian Lesslie Newbigin (whose book *Proper Confidence* I am deeply indebted to) writes, "We do not reach truth unless we allow ourselves to be exposed to, and drawn by, a truth that is beyond our present understanding."[10]

Scientists do this well. Through their curiosity, the language of science, their desire to know, and their willingness to submit to the data, they expose themselves to the possibility of discovering new truths.

For Polanyi, the discovery process often begins with a problem—but defining a problem can be difficult because problems lie at the nexus of the known and the unknown. In order to properly identify a problem, scientists intuit and investigate what is not yet fully seen. They imaginatively open themselves up to the new.

Commenting on pioneer astrophysicist Gerry Neugebauer's work in helping discover previously undetected galaxies, Dr. Thomas Soifer, the chair of physics, mathematics, and astronomy at Caltech, said, "Our imagination wasn't nearly as good as what the universe produces."[11] Most scientists would agree.

The imagination is crucial for grasping the unknown. "What has been written with imagination must also be read with imagination."[12] The scientific imagination is made in the image of a scientifically imaginative God.

Even as imagination is necessary for grasping the unknown, imagination plays a crucial role in compelling the need to know. The imagination is the first to believe there might be more going on than meets the eye. It nudges curiosity to investigate and dreams up

explanatory scenarios. These dreams create cognitive tension in the mind of the imaginer, further compelling the need to know.

Michael Polanyi believed that human beings know a lot more than they are able to explicitly formulate. He called this awareness "tacit knowledge." Lesslie Newbigin describes the concept this way:

> A boy of ten can ride a bicycle without being able to state explicitly the rules governing the relation between the turn he makes to keep his balance, the speed of the cycle, and the angle of disequilibrium. I can recognize my wife's face in a crowd of a thousand people, but I could not explicitly state the exact geometrical patterns of her features [that] enable me to do so. The explicit formulations of scientists rest upon this vast area of tacit knowledge which they share in greater or lesser degrees with all human beings.[13]

Just as scientists have tacit knowledge of the topics they study, human beings have tacit knowledge of God. This is part of the *sensus divinitatis* God has built into us, the part that makes an epiphany or discovery resonate like something we've always known or were meant to know. God has planted eternity into the human heart (Eccl. 3:11). Life is supposed to feel like we're unpacking what was intentionally put there. Even as everything that science will discover is already present in the universe, so too is God.

Imagine being reminded of this truth every time a new discovery is made, or new information is revealed.

RELATIONAL KNOWING

According to Newbigin, "The modern antithesis of observation and reason on the one hand versus revelation and faith on the other is

only tenable on the basis of a prior decision that the whole cosmic and human story has no purpose and therefore no meaning."[14] But we know the cosmic and human story do have purpose and meaning, and so we need to look beyond mere empirical and rational categories to rightly engage that reality.[15]

We all yearn for purpose and meaning. Our heartfelt question—*Why am I here?*—implies that Someone has the answer. Asking it is an act of faith we seemingly can't avoid. Eternity really has been planted into our hearts. When we seek purpose or meaning, we affirm that Someone has a purpose and meaning for our lives. We also affirm that we need that Person to reveal that purpose to us.

While science knows by way of empirical observation—the scientist objectively stands above what they are studying and draws rational conclusions—to discover one's purpose is to turn that process around. Purpose can only be known if it is revealed. Revelation can only come through the will of a revealer.

In order to know, we need to be addressed. Being addressed can happen even as we observe.

Separating revelatory knowing from empirical knowing is a false dichotomy. Think about how we know each other as human beings. Relational knowing is always a mix of both observation and revelation. Theologian Martin Buber delineated two kinds of knowing; the first where, "I am the masterful actor handling inert material which I am free to interrogate, to manipulate, and to organize, and . . . I am seeking to know another person who can resist my efforts to know and who can interrogate me and make me the object of inquiry."[16] These two ways of knowing need not stand opposed. To know the nature of reality is both to observe and to listen. For Newbigin, "In quantum physics, the observer and the object of observation do not belong to separate worlds; they interact."[17]

To truly observe you need to trust that what you're observing can

"speak." To engage the God of creation, you need to put your faith in the possibility that empirical knowing is connected to personal knowing. As St. Augustine wrote, "Crede ut intelligas," I believe in order to know.[18]

NEURON KNOWING

A while ago my son, a pre-med student, was standing in my living room teaching me how neurons communicate. For years he'd listened to my sermons on science-based topics; now it was his turn to preach.

My son told me that when neurons talk to each other across their synaptic gap (the space separating them), they communicate in a way that increases the capacity for communication to happen. He described how the actual physiology of neural connections increases with use. When neurons fire together, they wire together.

Neurons communicate with each other by having little packages fuse to their membranes that release chemicals between them. The very act of fusing these packages to the membrane thickens the communication branch of the cell, increasing the conduction potential of the communication "wire" by increasing its diameter.

In the process of learning and memory (in a specific area of the brain), two signals occurring in quick succession have a different effect than a single communication. Chemicals are released in the first signal that allow the second event to have a different impact on the receiving neuron, an impact that makes the second neuron *more* able to listen to the neuron it is connected to. One way a neuron can respond differently in a succession of communications is by sending a different message back to the first neuron. When the first cell receives this message, it increases the likelihood of further communication.

As my son explained, I found myself both observing and being

addressed. Through our back-and-forth dialogue, *we* were wiring together as father and son. Through our conversation, we were being known—by each other and by God.

The Bible teaches that true knowledge always leads to a changed life. When we commune with God, our capacity to commune with God increases. God responds to us, and we respond in return. The more we commune with God, the more God reveals. The more we fire together, the more we wire together.

Through my son's passion for neural connections, I came to understand more about the heart and mind of a God who seeks strong connections in all things. Even as we spoke about the physiology of the brain, my son and I were being spoken to. As we related to each other—speaking and listening, observing, and being observed—we knew each other more. Knowing each other more, we both knew and were being known by God.

None of these knowings came at the expense of the other. They weren't even different "levels" of knowing. They all just happened at the same time and were part of one synergistic whole.

Some thinkers create material/spiritual, objective/subjective, theory/practice dualisms, but God has no need for such dichotomies. In Jesus the material and spiritual come together perfectly; the objective becomes subject, and theory becomes reality.

FAITH-BASED KNOWING

According to Archbishop William Temple, "All faith is an experiment, and you cannot have the result of an experiment unless you make the experiment."[19]

Scientific knowing can come through faith or through what science calls *hypothesis*. A scientist posits what could be and then designs

an experiment to try to prove the hypothesis. Initially scientists intuit what can only be seen dimly and "affirm belief statements that can be doubted."[20] They imagine what *might be,* through faith.

Imagine that God personally self-reveals through what is empirically known. Let's make this our hypothesis. Theoretically it *is* possible—if you believe God created all things and wants to be known through what is made.

Given the significant amount of faith that science already presupposes, taking one more step of faith shouldn't be too much of a stretch. According to Abraham Kuyper,

> Science presupposes faith in self, in our self-consciousness; presupposes faith in the accurate working of our senses; presupposes faith in the correctness of the laws of thought; presupposes faith in something universal hidden behind the special phenomena; presupposes faith in life; and especially presupposes faith in the principles from which we proceed; which signifies that all these indispensable axioms, needed in a productive scientific investigation, do not come to us by proof, but are established in our judgment by our inner conception and given with our self-consciousness.[21]

Science already expresses faith in many ways.

In his book *Science and the Trinity,* John Polkinghorne writes about how scientists initially approach unknown realities. They start with broad categories—mapping the territory and identifying notable features—and then work toward a more detailed understanding, all within the context of what science already knows. These investigations are done with humility, "neither . . . too rationally overconfident nor totally tongue-tied."[22]

Theology operates in a similar way. For two thousand years the

church has tried to articulate the nature of a Jesus who is both human and God (both matter and spirit). While a detailed understanding of the incarnation remains elusive, the church's thought experiments have "thickened" their understanding of who Jesus is.[23] Mapping the gospel territory, theologians took note of how Jesus was conceived, His pre-birth existence, what He said about Himself, and how He acted. From there they came up with a theory of the incarnation they've been working on ever since.

Even as the church has done this with the incarnation, it can also do this with its attempts to understand how God personally reveals Himself through what is empirically known through science.

> *Revelation through Jesus has always been both cognitive and relational—at the same time. Jesus spoke about kingdom come, and He was kingdom come. He spoke words, and He was the Word.*

Following Polkinghorne, the thought experiment begins by believing enough to posit ideas more concrete than the facts can initially sustain.[24] Polkinghorne talks about quantum theory scientists skating on the thinnest of intellectual ice, "to the sound of cracking."[25] This initial step of faith is crucial for theorizing. If Jesus really is fully God and fully man, then it's entirely possible that relational-knowing is meant to occur alongside and through empirical-knowing. God revealed Himself through the incarnate Jesus, matter and spirit co-inhering. Jesus is the perfect image of God; He was presumably God's best way to show Himself to humankind. God is revealed personally through Christ. Revelation through Jesus has always been both cognitive and relational—at the same time. Jesus spoke about kingdom come, and He *was* kingdom come. He spoke words that were cognitively intelligible, and through those words He was the Word of God.

CREATIVE KNOWING

Polkinghorne goes on to talk about the importance of creativity in the faith/theorizing process. Even as theologians expend huge creativity imagining a God who takes on a human body, theoretical scientists express great creativity in stepping beyond the reasonable bounds of what they currently know. When the results of their creative theorizing bring new insight to present-day knowledge, their theories are bolstered and further developed.

> *Our need to know is insatiable because knowing about our world can lead us to knowing God.*

After centuries of theorizing about the incarnation, the church humbly articulated its best understanding of who Jesus was through the fourth-century Nicene Creed: "One Lord Jesus Christ, the only Son of God, begotten from the Father before all ages, God from God, Light from Light, true God from true God, begotten, not made; of the same essence as the Father. Through Him all things were made."[26] The Creed described Jesus as fully God and fully man at the same time, co-eternal with the Father, begotten, not made. Through the penultimate lens of the Nicene Creed, the gospel stories could then be read with greater clarity, thus affirming the incarnational theory as being on the right track.

Our need to know is insatiable because knowing about our world can lead us to knowing God. When physicists trace the history of the universe back to its beginnings, they can capture a glimpse of the Alpha and Omega. The truth science uncovers is iconic, a cognitive window through which humanity can see a God who is looking back at them.

Moving from Knowing to *Knowing*

The fact that you are now moving at 1.9 million mph relative to the rest of the universe is a good starting point for increasing your capacity to transform scientific-knowing into God-knowing.[27]

It starts with the realization that the perceived nature of reality is relative. From your perspective you're not moving right now, but from the perspective of someone who is looking at the universe as a whole you are. Both perspectives are true at the same time. Even as science has one understanding of a particular facet of the cosmos, God may have another.

Imagine applying this paradoxical truth to other knowing moments. Even as you perceive the nature of the object you're looking at as one thing, God may see it as another. You see it in part; God sees it in its wholeness. You see it at one point in time; God sees it from outside of time. You notice its attributes; God knows its purpose. Of course, you're both looking at the same thing, only from completely different perspectives.

This often happens in relation to other people. One person sees reality one way, and another person sees it another way. One scientist holds a theory while another holds a different one. Sometimes both are right, depending on your perspective. Could it be that paradoxes in perspectives are meant to point us to the fact that in any given situation God has a perspective as well? Knowing this can perhaps help you be more aware of God's presence everywhere.

PRACTICE

To get a glimpse of God's view of reality, we need to set our imaginations free. Even as we are able to look at the universe from outside of

the universe in order to imagine ourselves flying along at 1.9 million mph, we need to imaginatively step back if we want our perceptive horizons expanded.

One way to stretch our imaginations is to hold two seemingly disparate thoughts in our minds at the same time. Children may have good imaginations because the myelin sheaths on their neural circuits are thick and enable different thoughts about different things to be thought at the same time.[28] You need to become like a child to perceive the profound mysteries of God's revelation through creation. To the extent that your imagination can do this, you'll experience more of a "God's-eye view," which can then lead—through a movement of the Spirit—to a more God-present awareness.

Try to hold as many disparate things in your mind as you can. If you want to know God more through the scientific truths you encounter, don't let go of the awareness of how fast you're moving right now or of the trillions of DNA repairs going on in your body at this very moment. Imagine being one of the proteins making up the infinitesimal cascade of intercellular restoration. Imagine catching a ride on a neighboring galaxy and watching our galaxy fly on by. Imagine seeing the forces of tension and compression all playing out at the same time in your knee as you walk. Imagine a God who sees, sustains, and purposefully moves everything in the universe along. Even your deep desires and prayers are engaged by and responded to by God.

Another key to knowing God through scientific truths rests in your capacity to imaginatively engage and hold on to paradox. There are many paradoxical mysteries in the Scriptures. God is described as *three* in *one*. Jesus is both fully God and fully man. God is totally sovereign, and yet we have free will. We seek God; God seeks us. God's kingdom is here, but not yet. It's almost as though the ungraspable nature of these truths is intentional. We can't fully comprehend God

any more than we can fully comprehend the nature of the universe. Yet through Christ we're taught that we *can* know God. But even that knowing is filled with paradox—we know God in part even as we are known fully, now and not yet, in the stillness of this place, even as we are being hurled through the universe. This kind of knowing comes through a childlike imagination.

So practice being young again. Converse with people from different fields of expertise. Read a fantasy book. Listen to new music. Visit a museum or gallery. Read a biography of someone who did something you can't imagine doing. Walk in the forest. Draw an idea you're struggling with. Hang around with a child and play.

PRAY

Heavenly Father, make me think and believe like I'm young again. Vivify my atrophied imagination so I can see big things anew. Help me to ask why like a child asks why. Give me a childlike willingness to believe. Help me have the imaginative room for all You say, do, and are in this world.

CHAPTER SEVEN

GOD'S BEAUTY IN
DNA REPAIR MECHANISMS

A Word from Dustin Pearson

I HAVE BEEN TRAINING to be a scientist for twelve years, and it was during the early years of my bachelor's degree I became a Christian. Through a community that genuinely lived out their faith, I saw who God was and wanted Him in my life. Since making the decision to follow Christ, I have been attempting to live out my faith in that same manner, but I have always struggled to find ways to integrate my faith with my studies. Although I have been heavily involved in campus ministries, I still felt that when I was in the lab or classroom, my experience of God was limited, even nonexistent.

So when John asked me to take part in the process of revealing God's parables from my work on DNA repair, I was hesitant. I am not a theologian, and although I have taken steps to be more mindful and aware of God's presence in my work, I have never ventured to look for the deeper truths of God within the molecular. For me, it is easy to see God's presence resonate in the sunrise-lit mountains or within the harmonies of music, but my attention to His presence has never directed itself to my research.

Perhaps this lack of seeing was a function of being invested in a subject such that its wonder and beauty had become common, or perhaps it was simply a lack of trying to merge two main aspects of my character, that of Christ follower and that of scientist. It wasn't until I was asked to think about my work in DNA repair as more than an academic exercise that I could begin to see links. I began to see my research from a different perspective, to see the beauty of God's creation renewed in my mind. I remember one specific aspect of this process. John was interviewing me on DNA repair, and I was trying to explain a particularly complex process. As I talked, I began to lean in, becoming more animated and excited to share this amazing process with another person. John casually commented on my excitement, which I had not realized was happening. That made me pause. I was excited, very excited. I was reminded of *why* I choose to pursue this path. Most significantly, I realized I get to experience God's creation and see God reflected in my research. I got to see God's presence in my work.

Dr. Dustin D. Pearson completed his doctoral degree at the University of Calgary in 2021 and is currently one of the senior scientists in the Goodarzi laboratory and is the research operations manager for the Evict Radon National Study. His work focuses on the DNA repair biology of alpha particle exposure, as well as the study of the real-time indoor air dynamics of radon within the residential built environment. Dustin's graduate work was supported by the National Science and Engineering Research Council, the Achievers in Medical Science Doctoral Scholarship, and the Rejeanne Taylor Research Prize. Dustin's work is currently supported by the Canadian Cancer Society.

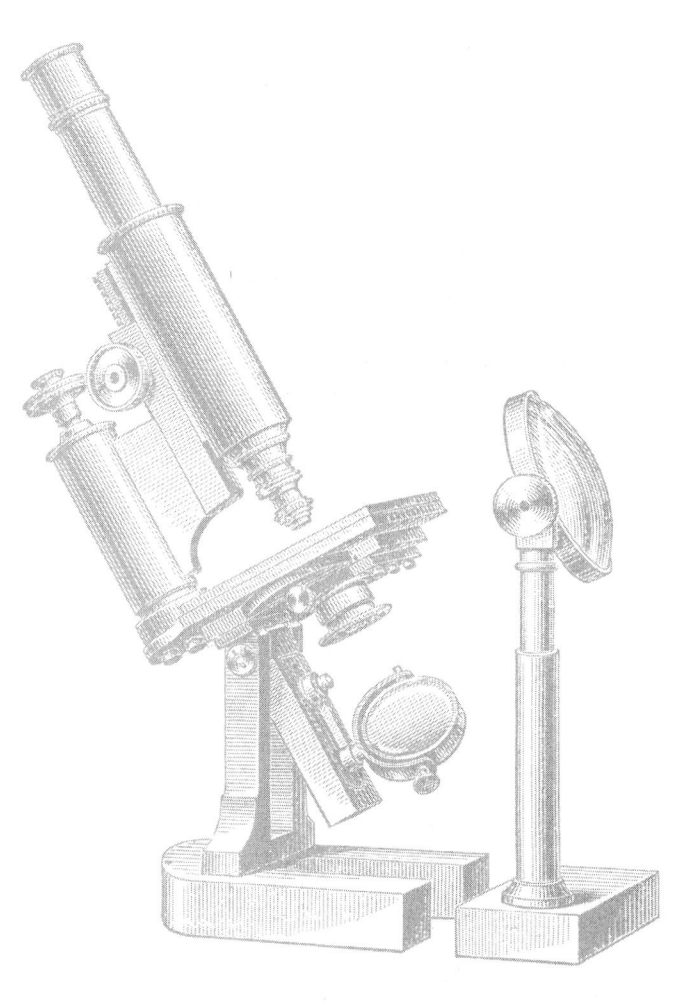

GOD'S BEAUTY IN DNA REPAIR MECHANISMS

*Beauty readily evokes a nameless yearning for
something more than earth can offer. . . .
Splendor reawakens our spirit's aching need for the infinite.*[1]

THOMAS DUBAY

DNA is the code that generates all the proteins our bodies need to function. If our DNA is damaged, this can lead to diseases such as cancer, neurological disorders, and even death.[2] Given the importance of this biopolymer, it is incredible to think that right now your DNA is being damaged and repaired tens of trillions of times per second. Within each of your 37.2 trillion cells,[3] it is estimated that there are thousands of repairs playing out per hour.[4] It is overwhelming to consider the immense scope of this unseen restorative work.

University of Calgary DNA researcher Dustin Pearson sees beauty in the complexity of the repair process:

Most of the enzymes involved in DNA repair have other functions in everyday cellular operation but are called into action

through a complex signaling cascade that not only knows what type of damage is present, but knows where in the cell's life cycle it is and calls for the appropriate repair at the right time. This all occurs through a dance of electrostatic interactions that, when enhanced through modification, attracts the right proteins/enzymes, or prevents the wrong proteins/enzymes from coming to the site of repair. This is all due to the efficient action of DNA repair.[5]

When you consider the immense saving power of this DNA bio-parable, it's hard not to join with the prophet Isaiah and exclaim, "Surely the arm of the LORD is not too short to save" (Isa. 59:1). Through countless preemptive repairs it's as though God is whispering, "Before they call I will answer; while they are still speaking I will hear" (Isa. 65:24).

God is continually healing us—and it's personal. The dance of electrostatic interactions comes from God's world-restoring imagination. God loves you in unseen and infinitesimal ways. DNA repair is not just a high frequency biological survival mechanism; it's a beautiful, God-given reminder that you are held. Your body isn't just a mass of self-sustaining cells to God—it's *you*.

The holiness that marks a human life is present in the DNA repair mechanisms that sustain it. The moment you begin to unpack the beauty of DNA repair, its glory begins to shine through. Writer Douglas Coupland writes, "It's so hard to balance in our minds the knowledge that 'the world' is mundanely 'a planet.' The former is so holy; the latter merely a science project."[6]

BEAUTY

Theologian Herman Bavinck wrote that "Beauty . . . evokes peculiar sensations and moods in human beings; it purifies our affections, reconciles the opposites in our life, brings harmony to the soul and bestows peace and rest."[7] When we consider the inestimable beauty of the complex workings of DNA repair, how can we not breathe a sigh of relief? We are being cared for in incredible and unseen ways right now—in ways that, if we let them, can lessen our anxieties and bring perspective, harmony, and peace.

Bavinck argues that beauty is experienced through "harmony, proportion, unity in diversity, organization, glow, glory, shining, fullness, [and] perfection."[8] One could apply all these words to the structures of DNA repair in the human body as well. Each attribute that Bavinck lists points us to God's nature. God's nature shines through beauty. Beauty catches our attention and evokes a wonder that leads to an experience of awe-inspired splendor and glory.

In the Bible, glory is conveyed as the "aspect in a person, or God, worthy of praise, honor, or respect."[9] Glory carries a sense of both holiness and splendor. In the Psalms, God's glory is often manifested through creation.[10] God's glory is revealed in saving acts described throughout the Scriptures, especially in the life and work of Jesus. Jesus is "glory's lamp, the reflection of glory, showing the true character of God."[11] Through the beauty of the person of Jesus and His saving works, humanity can see and experience the true character of God. To be fully human is to give God glory in all things—including our understanding of how DNA is repaired.

> **To be fully human is to give God glory in all things.**

John Calvin wrote, "We have been placed here, as in a spacious theatre, to behold the works of God [in creation], and there is no work of God so small that we ought to pass it by lightly, but all ought to be carefully and diligently observed."[12]

In his commentary on the book of Genesis, Calvin invites us to "Let the world become our school if we desire to rightly know God."[13] For Calvin, God was "a father 'inclined to allure us to himself by gentle and loving means,' one who created the world as a theatre of God's glory, using beauty to attract God's children in every possible way . . . Knowing God, for Calvin, was thus inescapably a matter of enjoying God."[14]

A primary focus of Dustin Pearson's DNA research is *Double Strand Breaks*. He describes these DNA breaks this way:

DNA is, of course, in two strands. If one strand is broken, that's easily repaired; but when two strands are broken, you get a separation of the genetic information, with the potential to lose information (one of the most toxic forms of damage). The kind of repair I deal with is non-homologous end joining, where a cascade of proteins come down and bind the ends of the broken and separated pieces of DNA and then bind them to each other. Then some other enzymes come and clean things up.[15]

The glory of this rebinding cascade echoes the glory of Christ's rebinding work. In a theological context, sin separates us from both God and each other. This separation is toxic. Jesus works in the gap, rebinding all the broken pieces of creation to God (Col. 1:18–20). One of the hallmarks of Jesus' reconnecting work is its mediating nature.

Pearson describes the breakdown process in more detail:

There's a very distinct process in non-homologous end join-ing. First on the scene are proteins called Ku 70 and 80, and they bind to the broken ends of the DNA. Then they act as a scaffold for another protein called DNA-PKcs; that comes and binds Ku. The DNA-PKcs on either broken end interact with each other, bringing the broken pieces together. Then several end-processing enzymes come along and clean up the ends of the DNA so they can be stuck together and form the new backbone of the DNA. The Double Strand Break is no longer a Double Strand Break.[16]

The standing-in-the-gap, Christlike, communal nature of this restorative pro-cess—a cascade of multiple proteins and enzymes—got me thinking about God's healing processes in a new way. As Chris-tians we often have a strong, Christ-cen-tered focus when we talk about God's work in the world of making things new,

> **While each person of the Trinity reveals something of the saving glory of God, together they reveal the fullness of God's saving glory.**

but God Himself is a community of persons—the Spirit, Jesus, and the Father—who each take on an individual role in the restorative process. While each person of the Trinity reveals something of the saving glory of God through their unique attributes, together they reveal the *fullness* of God's saving glory.

God's communal healing is clearly described in the words of the apostle Paul:

> For he himself [Jesus] is our peace, who has made the two groups (*Jew and Gentile . . . broken piece of DNA here and broken piece of DNA there*) one and has destroyed the barrier, the dividing wall of hostility . . . to reconcile both of them to

God through the cross, by which he put to death their hostility.
. . . For through him we both have access to the Father by one
Spirit. **EPH. 2:14–16,18,** *italics and additions mine*

Can you feel the electrostatic dance in this process?

While I've always known that each person of the Trinity played
a role in God's restoration process, I had never considered how intimately and interdependently they work. Could it be that when a
triune God heals, it's like a restorative cascade of proteins and enzymes arriving at the scene just in time, working in perfect sync, and
making all things new? This is the kind of synchronicity the apostle
Paul alludes to when he writes, "*God's* love has been poured out into
our hearts through the *Holy Spirit*, who has been given to us. You
see, at just the right time, when we were still powerless, *Christ* died
for the ungodly" (Rom. 5:5–6, emphasis mine).

We can no more save ourselves than we can repair our own
DNA. Right now, at a rate of tens of trillions of repairs per second,
God is reminding you of the breathtaking power of this amazing,
restorative grace.

Glimpsing God's DNA restoring glory is humbling and enliven-
ing. Second-century church father Irenaeus wrote, "The glory of God
is a human being fully alive; and to be alive consists in beholding
God."[17] When God shows us unmerited love physiologically through
DNA repair and we really see it for what it is, we are filled with wonder. It's as though the unseen work of DNA repair provides empirical
evidence for how wide and long and high and deep the love of Christ
is (Eph. 3:18). The beauty and wonder of DNA repair lead us into a
deeper appreciation of God's saving work and a greater awareness and
experience of God's presence, constantly working within us. Beauty
quickens our attention, wonder stills our souls, and then Christ pulls
back the veil. Could it be that every scientific experience of beauty

and wonder is meant to lead us to God in this way?

Describing DNA repair further, Dustin Pearson says, "The repair of DNA consists of both a *signaling* and *repair* axis. Without the proper functioning of these two separate axes (or functions), we do not get full repair of a single DNA break."[18] The moment a DNA break is detected, a signaling function stops cell reproduction and sends out a call for repair. Once the repair is completed, the cell continues in its healthy reproductive cycle. Signaling allows time for cell repair.

This dual nature of DNA repair reminds me of the necessity of Jesus' divine and human natures and how crucial it is that He is fully operative on both axes. Without Jesus being fully God and fully human, we could not get a full repair of our relational break with God. Perhaps the interrelated nature of the signaling and repair axes in DNA repair sheds some light on the mysteries of Christ's incarnate nature.

When I asked Pearson if there were any proteins in the cell that work on *both* axes—as signalers and repairers—he described an enzyme called ATM. ATM's *signaling* role is to make the signal strong enough to get a response, and its *repairing* role is to *modify* the "repair enzymes" it has signaled and to keep any unnecessary repair work from being done to the DNA. Simply put, ATM signals that there's a problem and then pitches in to help make the repair.

In seminary, I learned about the many early church councils that tried to put words around Jesus' *fully God* and *fully human* nature. They tried to encapsulate the mystery and complexity and necessity of Jesus being both at the same time. The church leaders knew that Jesus had to be fully human so He could fully know our human condition. They understood that Jesus had to be fully God, with all the necessary power to repair the breach, and with the wisdom to enable the healing to come in just the right way at the just the right time.

This ATM enzyme images its Maker—affirming that even at a molecular level Jesus is making all things new.

BEAUTY AND WONDER TAKE US THERE

When I first talk with scientists of faith about the possibility of experiencing God's revelation through their work, I am often puzzled by what I perceive to be the limiting effects of awe, wonder, and beauty. These means of engaging God seem to be the primary ways scientists experience God in their work. In conversation after conversation, I find myself trying to nudge them past these initial observations into a deeper, empirical, revelatory experience.

Now I realize I was operating under a false dichotomy. Beauty and wonder aren't walls—they're doors! Awe and wonder and beauty are the precise means God uses to draw our attention and take us deeper. They are a necessary first step into a richer engagement with God's splendor; they are more than enough on their own, but wonder and beauty carry a unique perception-widening capacity to take the observer further.

Human beings are made to marvel at creation. The Bible is filled with writers who do exactly that, and God calls us to do the same. The writer of Psalm 104 praises God for the workings of light, clouds, wind, water, thunder, mountains, valleys, springs, donkeys, birds, grass, cattle, wine, bread, oil, trees, storks, mountain goats, hyrax, the sun and moon, seasons, and lions. Then, as though realizing the list is endless, he writes, "How many are your works, Lord! In wisdom you made them *all*; the earth is full of your creatures" (Ps. 104:24, emphasis mine). The psalmist points to "the sea, vast and spacious, teeming with creatures beyond number—living things both large and small" (v. 25), then speaks of how God gives life and provision to

them all, wrapping up with these words of praise: "May the glory of the LORD endure forever; may the LORD rejoice in his works" (v. 31). The psalmist affirms that the created order is a means for revealing God's glory and that both human beings and God delight in the wonders of the cosmos. In fact, God rejoices in us as we rejoice in the beauty of creation.

When we're struck by the harmony, proportion, order, complexity, and inherent beauty of God's creation, and wonder and delight rise within us, we're experiencing what it means to be fully human. When science leads the way in these wonder-full regards, humanity is being fully humanity. Knowingly or not, everyone is worshiping God. In a way, Psalm 104 is a template for how science can help us worship God. The glories of creation connect us to a God who glories in creation. As we are taken by creation's beauty, God takes us and draws us near.

In an essay, Herman Bavinck wrote,

[Through an experience of beauty] God's glory meets and enlightens us in our perceptive spirits through the works of nature . . . Beauty is the harmony that still shines through the chaos in the world; by God's grace beauty is observed, felt, [and] translated . . . it is prophecy and guarantee that this world is not destined for ruin but for glory—a glory for which there is a longing deep in every human heart.[19]

The experience of beauty is not merely a subjective one. Father Thomas Dubay writes, "Both science and theology agree on the objectivity of beauty. While there is a subjective readiness in us, greater or lesser, for perceiving the splendid, both disciplines assume and insist that beauty is not merely in the eye of the beholder, it is primarily something 'out there.'"[20] While not everyone in the field of science

would agree, many do have a sense of beauty's "out there" nature.

God is out there, shining through beauty and engaging us through wonder. God wants to be known through all of creation's glories. This is what experiences of beauty and wonder can evoke. We're made to meet our Maker through our God-imaging, beauty-delighting ways. Beauty derives its content from things that are good and true, it's how good and true things make their appearance and reveal themselves.[21]

IN LOVE

In his book *The Evidential Power of Beauty*, Father Thomas Dubay writes about the connection between our desire for beauty and our desire for God. Through wonder and delight we are enriched and encounter truth and then, "capitulating to the truth," we fall in love. "Falling in love here does not refer to superficial infatuations or egocentric lust, but rather to a selfless commitment made to a fascinating beloved."[22] I wonder if this is the kind of love that inspires many scientists, a love that enables them to see and that fuels their commitment to their field of study (their fascinating beloved).

> **We're made to meet our Maker through our God-imaging, beauty-delighting ways.**

There is a Latin phrase used by the ancient mystics: *ubi amor, ibi oculus*, which means "Where there is love, there is seeing."[23] God is love. As Creator of the cosmos, God knows the real value and eternal significance of all that fills the universe. "With God nothing is empty of meaning," wrote the early church father Irenaeus.[24] Flipping this around: With God everything is *full* of meaning. God loves all of creation and made us to love it too. It's love that motivates God to restore creation to its former glory.

What was created in love is seen through love and restored in love.

Our ability to see God via creation is connected to our experience of true love. Learning about the unseen immensity of God's grace, especially reflected in repairing the break that separated us from God, gives us eyes and hearts to recognize God's love for all creation. To the extent that we know the wonder of Christ's love personally, we are able to engage and experience the wonder of His love externally, pulsing through the intricacies of creation.

> **Our ability to see God via creation is connected to our experience of true love.**

Love sees the elegance of what is loved.[25] Jesuit theologian Karl Rahner wrote that it enables us to become "permeable to and receptive of the deep meanings of things."[26] Love transforms us (through seeing God in creation) into our true selves. Love lets us see what's always been there.[27] To possess great love, we need to experience it. To see Christ's love in creation we need to intimately know Christ's love.

Love opens our eyes to God's beauty around us. St. Augustine stated it so eloquently:

> Late it was that I loved you, beauty so ancient and so new, late I loved you. And look, you were within me and I was outside and there I sought for you and in my ugliness I plunged into the beauties you have made. You were with me, and I was not with you. Those outer beauties kept me far from you, yet if they had not been in you, they would not have existed at all. You called, you cried out, you shattered my deafness; you flashed, you shone, you scattered my blindness; you breathed perfume, and I drew in my breath, and I pant for you; I tasted and I am hungry and thirsty; you touched me and I burned for your peace. [28]

LECTIO SCIENTIA

Experiencing Beauty More Deeply

All creation praises God. Like the sun, moon, and stars, human beings have a unique voice in the cosmic choir. Through science we can hear and are therefore able to harmonize with the creation voices that surround us.

If you've ever sung with a group of people (at church or at a concert), you know there is something about the engagement of surrounding voices that enables you to find your own voice. The voices of others encourage, complement, and carry yours.

PRACTICE

Imagine increasing your awareness of the creation-based voices that currently surround you. What if, the next time you feel the sun on your face, you "hear" its life-giving tone? Or if when you pass a tree you resonate with its remain-in-me rhythms? What if when you bend your knee you experience its made-to-move song? Imagine a life surrounded by these God-praising voices. You can't help *but* join in the song! These voices can shape and define your voice.

There isn't a part of God's good creation that isn't praising God right now. You just need ears to hear.

READ

The following Bible passage can help you hear. More than a few times Jesus pointed to a hearing beyond mere auditory perception. It's this kind of hearing that will enable you to attend to the creation choir:

He replied, "You've been given insight into God's kingdom. You know how it works. Not everybody has this gift, this insight; it hasn't been given to them. Whenever someone has a ready heart for this, the insights and understandings flow freely. But if there is no readiness, any trace of receptivity soon disappears. That's why I tell stories: to create readiness, to nudge the people toward a welcome awakening. In their present state they can stare till doomsday and not see it, listen till they're blue in the face and not get it. I don't want Isaiah's forecast repeated all over again:

Your ears are open but you don't hear a thing.
Your eyes are awake but you don't see a thing.
The people are stupid!
They stick their fingers in their ears
so they won't have to listen;
They screw their eyes shut
so they won't have to look,
so they won't have to deal with me face-to-face
and let me heal them.

"But you have God-blessed eyes—eyes that see! And God-blessed ears—ears that hear! A lot of people, prophets and humble believers among them, would have given anything to see what you are seeing, to hear what you are hearing, but never had the chance." **MATT. 13:11-17 MSG**

PRAY

Lord God Almighty, Maker of eyes and ears, attune us to the beauty of creation's song. Give us insight into every kingdom voice—all creatures great and small. Show us how creation works, and help us humbly take our place. Free our tongues to join the choir and sing Your praise forevermore.

CHAPTER EIGHT

NAMING CREATION VIA NEUROSCIENCE

A Word from a Neuroscientist

ONE OF THE THINGS that struck me, having young children, is how early they develop the ability to name things correctly from seeing the most abstract of drawings—even the ones attempted by their parents on the sidewalk with chalk. This is not imagination, although children are full of that too. It's an innate ability of the human brain to find analogies in all it sees. Our brains are designed to see anything and say, "Hey, this is like something I've seen before." How it does this is a magnificent thing. The central nervous system with its incredible sensory organs—retinal detectors and an optic nerve cascading into millions of synaptic computers and neural processors back and forth across our circuits—creates higher meaning out of squiggly lines.

In this chapter, Pastor John practices our God-given propensity for analogy with a unique perspective into the workings of our minds. What does neuroscience tell us about God? By uncovering and naming scientific truths here, can we find analogous truths about who God is? Pastor John recounts our conversations from a time near the end of the several years I spent intensely focused on deciphering a few thousand synapses onto

a few hundred neurons deep in the obscure inner caverns of the brain of a rat. Here, recordings of electrical current waves revealed retrograde signaling mechanisms gated by stress hormones in the hypothalamus. But what did it mean beyond the naming? Pastor John saw the biological equivalent of the Sabbath—a reminder that God's love will sustain and protect us through life's ordeals.

Finding analogies is not just core to how we learn about the world around us, but also important for how we learn about God. Naming is not just the practice of children. Pastor John works to reveal analogy as a core of spiritual cognition—by naming what we see, we can know God better.

8

NAMING CREATION VIA NEUROSCIENCE

Whatever the man called each living creature,
that was its name.

GENESIS 2:19

In the beginning God named the various parts of creation. Light was called "day" and darkness "night." God called the vault above the earth "sky," the dry ground "land," and the gathered waters, "seas" (Gen. 1:5, 8, 10). By naming creation God recognized, identified, and differentiated each part.

Because we are made in God's likeness, God calls us to continue to name creation: "The LORD God had formed out of the ground all the wild animals and all the birds in the sky. He brought them to the man to see what he would name them; and whatever the man called each living creature, that was its name. So the man gave names to all the livestock, the birds in the sky and all the wild animals" (Gen. 2:19–20).

God didn't compel man to name the animals, God just brought them to the man "to see what he would name them"—perhaps like a parent lets a child name a new pet. Man gave a name to each new animal. That name was a response to the creature's unique

being and was borne out of a heart that—like God's heart—seeks to bestow identity.

Reading the Genesis story, you get the sense that naming is an innate human response to newness. When we see something new, we need to know its name (like a child at the zoo). When we discover that a thing has no name, we feel compelled to provide one (like a zoologist with a new species). Every creature needs a name. Science understands this, and when science gives a name to a new discovery, perhaps that delights God.

NEURAL STRESS-REDUCING MECHANISMS

Years ago, a young neuroscientist in a church I was serving in uncovered something new about how brain cells communicate with one another during stress. For decades, her scientific forebearers theorized about the possibility of what she had now seen. Because they named what they saw, she was able to name what she saw. Naming enabled an understanding that became the foundation for future naming.

This young neuroscientist describes her scientific breakthrough:

> Traumatic or stressful experiences during critical windows of our lives, such as childhood or adolescence, can profoundly influence how resilient we will be to the challenges we face later on. The goal of my research is to understand how stress is processed by, and leaves an imprint on, our brains, particularly during these sensitive periods of time. I study a unique brain area called the hypothalamus, dedicated to regulating the release of stress hormones like cortisol and adrenaline. Through electrical recordings of rat brain-cell activity and communication, we can examine, with great detail, mechanisms that

govern neural processing of stress. By studying the brains of adolescent rats, I was able to uncover a brand-new way in which brain cells communicate during stress. I was able to observe how these cells in the hypothalamus can use substances—naturally produced versions of the active ingredients in painkillers like morphine (opioids)—as messengers to other brain cells. I found that opioids are made and released by cells to shut down communication lines. If you can imagine that during a stressful event many brain cells begin to panic and yell at one another, opioids are used by these particular cells to lower the volume or hang up the phone so that neurons don't become overwhelmed. What does this mean? Well, first, these findings help explain why teenagers might abuse opiate painkillers as a way of coping with stress. Second, it means our brains are more sensitive and flexible than we previously thought or could have imagined.[1]

This neuroscientist could not have given her discovery a name were it not for the work of earlier scientists who named the *brain, hypothalamus, hormones, cortisol, adrenaline, cells,* and *opioids.* Naming enabled the preservation and encapsulation of knowledge and opened the door to deeper inquiry. The moment someone named the brain, others began to ask questions about the brain's nature and to ponder its relationship to the rest of the body.

Through a long history of neural naming, science has brought us to a place where we have now begun to name this newly uncovered stress-regulating mechanism. By naming what God made, humanity can care for the brain more precisely using better targeted therapies and treatments.

Beyond these benefits, the very nature of this stress-reducing mechanism reflects who God is. In the Old Testament book of Isaiah,

God says, "When you pass through the waters, I will be with you; and through the rivers, they shall not overwhelm you" (Isa. 43:2 ESV). When God addresses Job in his time of stress, God asks, "Who shut up the sea behind doors when it burst forth from the womb, when I made the clouds its garment and wrapped it in thick darkness, when I fixed limits for it and set its doors and bars in place, when I said, 'This far you may come and no farther; here is where your proud waves halt'?" (Job 38:8–11). God promises to keep chaos at bay. This newly discovered neural stress-reducing mechanism is one way that God—physiologically—keeps this promise.

God is the one who first named (knew the nature of) this neural stress-reduction process. Knowing in advance that humanity was going to encounter a lot of stress and experience a lot of brokenness, God gave us an "out"—a way to buy some time. Through the naming of this neural gift, we can now develop new drugs and treatments to help us better cope with stress.

This stress-reduced space is a kind of Sabbath, "a period of non-responsiveness you need to recover. The opioids take you away from that place where you can't respond effectively."[2] Sabbath takes us away from a place where we can't respond effectively to a place with God where we can slow down, breathe, and remember that God is the one who keeps us safe. Sabbath is where we are reminded that God's saving work is not dependent on our decisions—no more than our neural stress-reducing mechanisms are. Through the gift of Sabbath, we can know who we are again and gain new perspective.

Now that science has named this newly discovered stress-reducing mechanism, it has gained new perspective. Scientists can now stand on what they know and see a little further ahead—and even, perhaps, to look back and see more clearly how they got there.

The act of naming reality can be prophetic in a way. Science names what God already knows. In the Bible, prophecy operated

in two ways. Prophecy clearly articulated the present state of affairs, and it also named a not-yet-clearly seen future. Prophets named what God already knew about the errant ways of God's people, their need to repent, and a future redemptive plan that would come through Christ. Often these two facets of naming—present and future—were intermingled. What was named for a certain time and place, with the limited knowledge a prophet had, also contained foreknowledge of the future name and nature of Christ. Even as Christ was mysteriously present in prophecies that preceded Him, so too was this newly discovered stress-reducing mechanism present long before it was actually seen. Perhaps earlier neuroscientists had a hunch that this kind of stress-saving mechanism was already present; even as they named what they knew at their time.[3]

Perhaps this is the nature of all truth: it fits with what preceded it, aligns with the current data, and then points to a greater future understanding of itself. What's true in relation to the revelation of Christ in the Bible is true of the revelatory nature of neural stress-reducing mechanisms in the human brain (made through Christ).

> *Knowing Jesus' name, we can get a sense of where God is taking creation and catch a glimpse of the heaven-on-earth perfection God has in mind.*

This concept fits with the way God progressively takes on new "names" in the Bible. In the beginning God was Creator. Then, through the exodus, God took on the name Deliverer. Through the giving of laws, God was affirmed as Holy. Through countless acts of forgiveness, God's name was recognized as Redeemer. God's unfolding Old Testament names are most clearly pronounced in the New Testament name Jesus. Jesus is Creator, Deliverer, Holy, and Redeemer. He is the embodiment of these names given to God throughout the Old Testament.

Knowing Jesus' name, we can now stand on it and see further ahead and also behind. We can get a sense of where God is taking creation and catch a glimpse of the heaven-on-earth perfection God has in mind. Through Christ, we can begin to see earth as it is meant to be, in the fullness of its name. Through Christ, our imaginations can be kindled by the thought that one day on the new heaven-on-earth, we'll know more and more about God's name forever.

Perhaps part of that eternal knowing of God's name will come through our ongoing naming and knowing of the created order. Conceivably, we could be naming the mysterious nature of the human brain for all eternity.

THE PURPOSE OF NAMING

Naming creation is crucial for human flourishing. Where would penicillin and yeast be if it weren't for the earlier discovery and naming of fungi? The more science names, the more we know and are able to care for and benefit from what God has made.

Naming is crucial for knowing. According to taxonomist Dr. Camilo Mora, "You cannot have any understanding of the ecology—the role—that a species has [unless] you have a name [for] them."[4] Naming gives all the species a place in the overall ecosystem—a rightful place (now that they have been seen), an important place (because they must be there for a reason), and a unique place (because there is no other exactly like them).

When science names the nature of reality, humanity gains a deeper appreciation of the depth and breadth of God's good creation. The more we name creation for what it is, the more we can know God for who God is.

KNOWING GOD IN THE NAMING

God knows the name of everything: "Every animal of the forest is mine, and the cattle on a thousand hills. I know every bird in the mountains, and the insects in the fields are mine" (Ps. 50:10–11) and "[God] determines the number of the stars and calls them each by name" (Ps. 147:4).

In a more complete sense than we can imagine, God knows the true nature and name of everything that exists—what it is, how it fits, where it came from, and where it's going. In the Bible, to know the name of something or someone was to know "the essential nature of its bearer; to know the name is to know the person."[5] God knows our names, and through Jesus we know God's name. The glory of this reality led

> **Every human, animal, plant, and chemical family derives its name from God.**

the apostle Paul to exclaim, "For this reason I kneel before the Father, from whom every family in heaven and on earth derives its name" (Eph. 3:14–15).

Every human, animal, plant, and chemical family derives its name from God. All that God has named reflects something of God's thinking and glory, and in accordance with their name and nature they give glory back to God. "All the earth worships you and sings praises to you; they sing praises to your name," wrote the psalmist (Ps. 66:4 ESV). Sun, moon, and stars praise God (Ps. 148). When science names created things for what they are, humanity is in a better place to glorify God through their creation-naming work. God wants to be known in the naming.

In a 2009 TED Talk, University of California researcher Dr. Vilayanur Ramachandran described the nature of mirror neurons, a subset of motor neurons that fire when we observe the actions

of another: "So here is a neuron that fires when I reach and grab something, but it also fires when I watch Joe reaching and grabbing something. And this is truly astonishing because it's as though this neuron is adopting the other person's point of view. It's almost as though it's performing a virtual reality simulation of the other person's action."[6]

Our brains utilize this neural mirroring to learn how to emulate complex actions. Dr. Ramachandran posits that long ago there was a

> sudden emergence of a sophisticated mirror neuron system, which allowed [us] to emulate and imitate other people's actions. . . . When there was a sudden accidental discovery by one member of the group, say the use of fire, or a particular type of tool, instead of dying out, this spread rapidly, horizontally across the population, or was transmitted vertically, down the generations.[7]

What if God created mirror neurons in part so that we could imitate the creation-naming actions of others? Just as scientists build on the naming work of their predecessors, human culture builds on the naming work of others. Mirror neurons enable us, in part, to appropriate and apply what others have clearly named. The whole of the naming network that makes up humanity is immense—a planet full of people naming more and more of what makes up our seemingly infinite world. All this naming collectively images a universe-naming God. When a scientist names something new they can mirror the God who made them.

Surely God takes pleasure in knowing the name of every thing. When a scientist delights in naming something for the first time, they mirror God's delight. In appreciating the fullness of something for what it is, scientists catch a better glimpse of a God's-eye view of

reality. When they see and name things God already knows, God is near. The honor and delight experienced by the scientist through the naming process is an honor and delight God feels for the scientist in that naming moment.

Scientists can also mirror God's sense of ownership when they name things. To name something is to know that thing. To know that thing is to possess something of it. In a very real sense, all great scientific breakthroughs *belong* to the scientist who made the discovery—and gave it a name. Special relativity belongs to Einstein, the helical structure of DNA to Watson and Crick, and gravitational waves to the scientists at LIGO.[8] The goodness of this naming/belonging phenomenon brings the scientist closer to a God to whom the universe really *does* belong. God can be known in the feeling of shared ownership.

When scientists name things, they can mirror God's gathering heart. God's master plan is to gather up *all things* in Christ: "With all wisdom and insight he has made known to us the mystery of his will, according to his good pleasure that he set forth in Christ, as a plan for the fullness of time, to gather up all things in him, things in heaven and things on earth" (Eph. 1:8–10 NRSVCE). When something has a name it can be called and then gathered in. When science names a facet of physical reality, it brings definition to the cosmic scope of God's gathering plan. The more we name, the more we're humbled by the remarkable extent of God's all-encompassing saving wisdom. Every name is one of an infinite number of names. The gratification a scientist may experience in naming and gathering in a new species, molecule, or neural stress-reduction mechanism is akin to the gratification God felt in originally naming these things into being. In a like-minded way, both the scientist and God love it when all things are seen for what they truly are and find their rightful place.

WHERE NAMING FALLS SHORT

But a name can never fully capture the essence or identity of a thing. As the young neuroscientist told me, the "number of permutations and combinations of brain activity exceeds the number of elementary particles in the universe."[9]

Ask a gut microbiome scientist to summarize the inner workings of the trillions of bugs that make up the human microbiome and you're likely to be answered with a very long pause. Astrophysicists cannot definitively tell us how many stars, or galaxies for that matter, make up our universe. In many ways it seems words like *brain*, *microbiome* and *universe* are just too small.

> **While we need naming to get us anywhere, it cannot get us everywhere.**

While we need naming to get us anywhere, it cannot get us everywhere. It's the same when it comes to knowing God. By nature, God is unnamable. God's thoughts are beyond ours, and God's ways unfathomable. God is outside time and space. God simply is. The Bible can't contain God any more than a universe can. God's name—God's essential nature—is beyond pronunciation. While we can enter the throne room of God through the name of Jesus, I'm not sure that when we get there, that we'll *ever* fully know God's name.

But that doesn't mean we shouldn't try.

Even as church liturgies, practices, and the Bible create a framework for engaging the name of God, all that science is and has named so far gives us a framework for knowing God through the book of creation.

"We will never, ever, really understand how neurons work," my neuroscientist friend said. She went on,

It doesn't matter how technology advances or how many decades of research pass, or how many paradigm shifts occur in our thinking. But this doesn't make the process of learning about neurons feel futile or daunting (although some days we simply answer our research questions with "the brain is complicated"). Quite the opposite: everything I learn makes neuronal communication more elegant, more beautiful, and more mysterious. Trying to understand God: his power, his plans, his mercy, his love . . . it's kind of the same deal.[10]

Again, naming frameworks give us something to stand on and enable us to see just a little bit further and with more clarity.

I find it affirming that the things science names fit together. In a 2007 TED Talk, Nobel Prize–winning physicist Murray Gell-Mann talks about Isaac Newton's assertion that nature conforms to herself: "A trivial example is this: Newton found the law of gravity . . . Coulomb, in France, found the same law for electric charges . . . You look at gravity, you see a certain law. Then you look at electricity; sure enough [it's] the same rule. . . . There are lots of more sophisticated examples."[11]

This idea of "nature conforming to herself" is very much like the church's view of the Scriptures. If you want to understand (name) a particular Bible passage, read it in its broader context; the surrounding context should affirm and illuminate the passage. God's revelation through the Bible conforms to itself even as God's revelation through nature conforms to itself. If you look at the Old Testament priestly order and sacrificial system, you'll see a prototype of Jesus' New Testament priestly sacrifice. Like scientists today, the Bible's writers named, to the best of their ability, what they were able to see. Each gospel writer wrote a unique account of who Jesus was, and all four accounts conformed to each other. Together they give us a more

complete picture of who Jesus is—of what His name is.

You can trust that when you name what you can—with whatever knowledge you have—the overall system (be it nature, the Bible, or the field of science) will do its affirming/conforming work. In God's universe, everything fits:

> So spacious is [Jesus], so expansive, that everything of God finds its proper place in him without crowding. Not only that, but all the broken and dislocated pieces of the universe—people and things, animals and atoms—get properly fixed and fit together in vibrant harmonies, all because of his death, his blood that poured down from the cross. **COL. 1:19-20 MSG**

A good name fits with what is named. A good name also fits with what science already knows. Everything that fills the universe is meant to find its proper place in Christ. The good fit of a subatomic, taxonomic, or geophysical theory is resonant with this greater good fit. All the good names that we've come up with fit and find their proper place within the name of Jesus. The goodness of science's naming of reality fits within the goodness of Jesus' name, character, and being.

In the beginning God created human beings with reason, curiosity, and an amazing capacity to figure out how things work. As people began to study, unpack, and name the physical cosmos, they called their work science. When science grew in proportion to the immense complexities of the universe, scientists specialized so they could give each field of study more specific attention. Soon there were thousands of different kinds of scientists—astrophysicists, nephrologists, botanists, and cytologists. Each became expert at naming the nature of their specialty and each uniquely images God's world-making mind.

LECTIO SCIENTIA

Knowing God in the Naming

Naming is the place where the *parable of scientist* and *icon of creation* meet. In the naming moment, God's revelation through the image-bearing nature of a scientist enters into a formal relationship with God's revelation through what is being named. Both parties to the naming transaction become more fully themselves at a creation-naming moment. This is what a neuroscientist is made to do. This is what neurons are.

There's something holy about this naming process. When God's creatures are most fully themselves, God's presence can be felt.

Of course, God is always present. God loves this world and knows every creature's name. As parents are delighted when someone remembers their child's name, God is delighted when we recognize creation for what it is. God rejoiced when science first got its name. When science acts in ways that are fully itself, God is overjoyed. When humanity names the gift of science, it glorifies the name of the Giver and, in so doing, does something more.

"Words and gestures of praise," theologian Catherine La Cugna writes, "are 'performative'; their utterance makes *actual* the glory of God to which they refer."[12] For Augustine, Luther, and Calvin, preaching was understood to be an act where God literally speaks through the words of a sermon.[13] If naming is a part of God's calling for humanity, then surely the naming process has a similar authority, making *actual* the glory of God to which it refers. When science names reality for what it is (insofar as it gets it right), God is, in a real sense, speaking. When something is authoritatively named, its now-acknowledged presence points to an even greater Presence.

PRACTICE

What if, when you encounter a newly named scientific reality, you stop and ponder its name? Ask yourself why it was given the name it was. Take note of how the name fits, how it captures some facet of the essence of what's being named. Then take that essence and use it as a lens. Look through it to see if there is something new about the nature of God you've not previously considered. Thank God for the new insight. Then consider the scientist who did the naming. What gave them the authority to choose that name? How does their scientific authority help you better understand God's scientific authority, God's universe-conceiving mind?

Theologian Walter Brueggemann describes the creation psalm, Psalm 104, as an act of worship that "calls into being the world God requires." The psalm's naming words are "not only responsive, but also . . . *constitutive*." They create what they name.[14]

Imagine engaging science through this kind of constitutive lens. Nature-naming scientists re-bring into being all that God initially brought into being. With every naming act, they image their Creator.

READ

Praise the LORD, my soul.

LORD my God, you are very great;
   you are clothed with splendor and majesty.

The LORD wraps himself in light as with a garment;
   he stretches out the heavens like a tent
   and lays the beams of his upper chambers on their waters.
He makes the clouds his chariot
   and rides on the wings of the wind.
He makes winds his messengers,
flames of fire his servants.

He set the earth on its foundations;
    it can never be moved.
You covered it with the watery depths as with a garment;
    the waters stood above the mountains.
But at your rebuke the waters fled,
    at the sound of your thunder they took to flight;
they flowed over the mountains,
    they went down into the valleys,
    to the place you assigned for them.
You set a boundary they cannot cross;
    never again will they cover the earth.

He makes springs pour water into the ravines;
    it flows between the mountains.
They give water to all the beasts of the field;
    the wild donkeys quench their thirst.
The birds of the sky nest by the waters;
    they sing among the branches.
He waters the mountains from his upper chambers;
    the land is satisfied by the fruit of his work.
He makes grass grow for the cattle,
    and plants for people to cultivate—
    bringing forth food from the earth:
wine that gladdens human hearts,
    oil to make their faces shine,
    and bread that sustains their hearts.
The trees of the LORD are well watered,
    the cedars of Lebanon that he planted.
There the birds make their nests;
    the stork has its home in the junipers.
The high mountains belong to the wild goats;
    the crags are a refuge for the hyrax.

He made the moon to mark the seasons,
    and the sun knows when to go down.
You bring darkness, it becomes night,
    and all the beasts of the forest prowl.
The lions roar for their prey
    and seek their food from God.
The sun rises, and they steal away;
    they return and lie down in their dens.
Then people go out to their work,
    to their labor until evening.

How many are your works, Lord!
    In wisdom you made them all;
    the earth is full of your creatures.
There is the sea, vast and spacious,
    teeming with creatures beyond number—
    living things both large and small.
There the ships go to and fro,
    and Leviathan, which you formed to frolic there.

All creatures look to you
    to give them their food at the proper time.
When you give it to them,
    they gather it up;
when you open your hand,
    they are satisfied with good things.
When you hide your face,
    they are terrified;
when you take away their breath,
    they die and return to the dust.
When you send your Spirit,
    they are created,
    and you renew the face of the ground.

May the glory of the LORD endure forever;
  may the LORD rejoice in his works—
he who looks at the earth, and it trembles,
  who touches the mountains, and they smoke.

I will sing to the LORD all my life;
  I will sing praise to my God as long as I live.
May my meditation be pleasing to him,
  as I rejoice in the LORD.
But may sinners vanish from the earth
  and the wicked be no more.

Praise the LORD, my soul.

Praise the LORD. **PS. 104**

PRAY

Lord, speak my name. Bring me into being. Create my life anew. Help me know who I am so that I can step into Your world-naming calling in a way that always honors You.

CHAPTER NINE

GOD'S HYDROLOGICAL HEART IN A RIVER

A Word from Masaki Hayashi

WATER IS ESSENTIAL to our physical being; very few plants and animals can sustain life without it. Natural water is in a continuous loop called by scientists "the hydrologic cycle." As John mentions in this chapter, Scripture often observes the hydrologic cycle. My favorite is Ecclesiastes 1:7: "All streams flow into the sea, yet the sea is never full. To the place the streams come from, there they return again."

I am a scientist who studies hidden parts of the hydrologic cycle in a form of groundwater. We only get to see groundwater in action when it springs up to the surface. Yet great rivers and awesome waterfalls all start with a trickle of water coming out of headwater springs high up in the mountains or in the middle of the prairie fields. John reminds us that our life is like that too. We are blessed by tiny little graces of God appearing out of many places, most of them hidden from our view. We are all part of the great cycle of grace that goes around and comes around.

Dr. Masaki Hayashi is a professor at the Department of Geoscience, University of Calgary. He studies groundwater and its connection with rivers, lakes, wetlands, and the atmosphere.

9

GOD'S HYDROLOGICAL
HEART IN A RIVER

"I will make rivers flow on barren heights."
ISAIAH 41:18

Years ago, I preached a sermon on the waters of the Bow River that flow from Alberta's Rocky Mountains all the way to Hudson Bay.[1] This river brings life to the many cities, towns, farms, and creatures along its path.

Over the past two decades, there have been many news stories written about the potential impact of climate change on the Bow River. One of the concerns lies with the melting mountain snowpack. When global temperatures rise, snow may melt too quickly in the spring and leave late-summer river flow rates at perilously low levels.

As part of my sermon research, I met with Dr. Masaki Hayashi, a Canada Research Chair in Geoscience at the University of Calgary. Through Dr. Hayashi, I learned that 80 percent of the water that fills the Bow River is groundwater; most of what sustains so many comes from an unseen subterranean source. This unseen source reminded me of an invisible Spirit that keeps all things and never runs dry. Jesus once promised, "Whoever believes in me, as Scripture has said, rivers

of living water will flow from within them" (John 7:38).

In 2006, Dr. Hayashi made an amazing discovery. Studying the inflows and outflows of Lake O'Hara—a lake high in the Rocky Mountains—he stumbled upon an inconsistency: the inflows from surface water sources were significantly less than the lake's outflows. How could this be? With further study, Dr. Hayashi realized what was going on—there was groundwater in the Rocky Mountains *above* the tree line! Until this time hydrologists had only known about groundwater *below* the tree line.

Dr. Hayashi describes the implications of his discovery for the Bow River:

> In the highest part of the Rocky Mountains the peak snow melt is in late June or early July. If this snowmelt water came out very quickly then we would have a lot of water coming down the mountain in a few weeks and not much left afterward. A sizable fraction of snowmelt water and glacier melt percolates into the rocks and sediments and becomes part of groundwater. The groundwater remains in the rocks and sediments for a few weeks to a few months and slowly comes out to streams and maintains the flow during the summer and the fall. This is like storing snowmelt and glacier melt in a bucket with a slow leak. The bucket can buffer the effects of climate warming; for example, an earlier timing of snow melt, or more rain and less snow in early spring.[2]

God has built a modulating safeguard into the Rocky Mountains so that if glacial or snow melt happens too quickly or too soon the mountains will hold the water and release it in a trickle so the late-season river doesn't run dry.

In the Bible we read, "I [God] will make rivers flow on barren

heights" and "[God] brought streams out of a rocky crag and made water flow down like rivers" (Isa. 41:18; Ps. 78:16). Like geophysical mountain buckets, God's grace is hidden in unseen places throughout the universe, just waiting to be discovered. God is whispering words of love through the matter-expanding nature of supernovae, the unmerited miracle of DNA repair, and the beauty and brilliance of high-mountain hydrology.

And God's word will not return to God empty:

> As the rain and the snow
>   come down from heaven,
> and do not return to it
>   without watering the earth
> and making it bud and flourish,
>   so that it yields seed for the sower and bread for the eater,
> so is my word that goes out from my mouth:
>   It will not return to me empty,
> but will accomplish what I desire
>   and achieve the purpose for which I sent it.
> You will go out in joy
>   and be led forth in peace;
> the mountains and hills
>   will burst into song before you. **ISA. 55:10-12**

GOD'S WORD THROUGH SCIENCE

Over the past century, God has used science to uncover countless creation-based truths. Christians now have more with which to know God than ever before. Yet because we have failed to grasp the revelatory weight of these scientific truths, we've missed out on a lot

of what God is saying and it has limited our capacity to steward creation wisely.

Because we don't fully know what God is thinking, we don't fully know how to act. This has left us with a world where corporations abuse ecosystems, scientists falter ethically, churches ignore God's environmental data, and people everywhere aimlessly search for their place in the cosmos.

I have argued that human beings are made to know God through two books—the Bible and creation. When we engage creation through the lens of the Scriptures, we can know that the universe is God's creation and science is God's brainchild. Both image God— the universe in its infinite complexity and science in its matter-mattering, providentially intervening, wholly interdependent, empirically minded, creation-naming, and beauty-appreciating ways.

Imagine a world where the church and science see each other as indispensable allies in the pursuit of knowing God; each realizing they need the other's map of reality.

British philosopher Mary Midgley says that to rightly engage the "most important questions in human life, a number of different conceptual tool-boxes . . . have to be used together."[3] We need "multiple maps of reality" to understand the true nature of any matter.[4] The question of *who God is and how we are to live before God* is surely the most pressing matter for any human being; one that science and theology together can help answer.

Imagine a world where the church and science see each other as indispensable allies in the pursuit of knowing God, each realizing they need the other's map of reality to fully understand the truth. Imagine a world where science and faith come together in a mutually interdependent, humble, and synergistic way.

So much could change for scientists if they met God at work! And once the church experienced God through science, it could learn to embrace all that science brings in relation to unpacking God's revelation through creation.

What's beautiful about this idea is that both science and the church could grow in knowledge through the *same* discoveries—with new hydrological truths increasing our understanding of the nature of both mountain-fed rivers and the grace God has hidden in creation. New discoveries can feed two bodies of knowledge—scientific and theological.

In this kind of world, we would have more godly wisdom to help us engage the moral, ethical, and theological challenges we face. To the extent that the church and science can experience God through what science reveals, they can both be closer to each other and to God. In that more intimate place, they can possess more of God's humility, perspective, and understanding.

This can begin to happen through a deeper engagement of God's revelation through creation.

HOW COULD IT WORK?

When science and faith co-experience God through creation, they can better steward our world. We've already caught a glimpse of how that might work.

As humanity engages the *empirical mind of God* as it is imaged through both scientists and scientific processes (thinking God's thoughts after God), we'll be reminded of the origin and purpose of our capacity to reason. Knowing we were created to know the mind of Christ, we can discipline our thinking, study well, and speak and act with God-honoring wisdom. Knowing that God thoughtfully created

all things will keep us from thoughtlessly intervening in creation.

As we recognize just how much matter matters to God and as we experience God in matter-mattering moments, we'll treat creation with renewed reverence. Knowing the provenance of all things—where matter comes from and where it's going—we'll be compelled to handle it with greater care.

When we engage the immense scope of God's providentially intervening presence in creation (as mirrored and illuminated through the providential interventions of science) we'll be humbled and encouraged to take up our providentially intervening roles. Understanding that we can come to know God through our actions, we can choose to do what's right—because it is right and because by doing it right, we'll be in sync with God's way of intervening. Experiencing God's providential sovereignty will make us more responsible as human stewards.[5]

When science points to creation's interdependent nature, we can be reminded of an interdependent God and be compelled to tread lightly in our intervening acts. We'll know we can't naively pull a thread or throw something into the universal equation without consequence. Science has proven countless times that everything is connected; every action has both known and unknown consequences.

Our experiences of beauty, awe, and wonder can also have a profound impact on our moral decision-making. There is a love that attends the appreciation we feel when we are moved by beauty—a love that leaves a deep impression. As human beings, made to love the world as God does, we have been given an innate capacity to see beauty in all things. Beautiful NASA images of the universe, incredible genetic discoveries, and elegant quantum theories evoke a love that points to a Love. When we consider God's love for what we appreciate, our love grows, enabling us to see even more beauty. The more beautiful we see our world—the more loved, appreciated, and cared for it will be.

When science gives a name to what it discovers, we'll have an opportunity to remember our name as "human beings"—called to steward creation in Godlike ways and to responsibly fill the earth with people, technology, and society. Even as naming "makes actual the glory of God," we can know that it also, in a sense, re-creates reality. Naming is a process that re-sees, or sees again for the first time, what is being observed. The moment something has a name it's not easily forgotten. Even as a mother can never forget her child's name, so too should we not forget our duty of care toward God's creation.

By knowing God through creation, through all of these means, we'll know how to be human in this world. Our actions, ethical choices, environmental decisions, and theological assertions can be shaped by God's real presence in creation. Our propensity to wield power in self-serving, idolatrous, or inappropriate ways will be tempered as we stand before God's inestimable power. Our search for purpose and meaning will begin to find its answer in the face of a God who made and sees us all.

A PROPHETIC WAY FORWARD

In the Old Testament book of Jeremiah, the prophet made a series of prophecies about God's promises to us, each founded on God's faithfulness in creation.

This is what the LORD says,

> he who appoints the sun
> to shine by day,
> who decrees the moon and stars
> to shine by night,

> who stirs up the sea
> so that its waves roar—
> the LORD Almighty is his name:
> "Only if these decrees vanish from my sight,"
> declares the LORD,
> "will Israel ever cease
> being a nation before me."

This is what the LORD says:

> "Only if the heavens above can be measured
> and the foundations of the earth below be searched out
> will I reject all the descendants of Israel
> because of all they have done,"
> declares the LORD. **JER. 31:35-37**

This pattern repeats itself in the next two chapters. Jeremiah prays, "Sovereign LORD, you have made the heavens and the earth by your great power and outstretched arm. Nothing is too hard for you. You show love to thousands" (Jer. 32:17–18), and he declares, "This is what the LORD says, he who made the earth, the LORD who formed it and established it—the LORD is his name: 'Call to me and I will answer you and tell you great and unsearchable things you do not know'" (Jer. 33:2–3), and he reminds us, "If you can break my covenant with the day and my covenant with the night, so that day and night no longer come at their appointed time, then my covenant with David my servant—and my covenant with the Levites who are priests ministering before me—can be broken" (Jer. 33:20–21).

God draws a direct line between the power that sustains the universe and the power that sustains God's people. God connects the moral actions that uphold the cosmos to the moral actions that uphold God's people.

Through Jeremiah, God reminds us that creation is a credible witness—offering clear evidence of God's trustworthiness. And if God's actions in upholding the universe can be trusted (including the promise to hold and direct our lives), then surely our capacity to act faithfully in *our* decision-making will be impacted.

God faithfully sustains all things—the cosmos, God's people, and their actions. The very fact of our ongoing universe ("Only if these decrees vanish from my sight") proves that God can be trusted to do the right thing. Facts that science uncovers also suggest this is true: "Only if hundreds of billions of galaxies cease to exist, and all matter disappears, and molecular bonds fail, will I ever cease to do the right thing and care for you."

> **God reminds us that creation is a credible witness—offering clear evidence of God's trustworthiness.**

The unending mysteries of the universe ("Only if the heavens above can be measured and the foundations of the earth below be searched out") point to an infinitely wise Maker and confirm that only God knows all the answers. Science can't ever know all the answers, but we can be assured that the God who already knows all things has the answers in hand. God knows what everything is, why it's here, and where it's going. God knows who you are, why you're here, and where you're going.

The sheer power displayed through God's creation of all things ("You have made the heavens and the earth by your great power and outstretched arm") is proof that nothing is too hard for God. God shows love to thousands—to billions—and works for the good of others so they can have life in abundance. God's power, as evidenced in the universe, reminds us that true power acts selflessly. The Power that sustains the cosmos—our home—calls us to use power in universe-sustaining ways. When we wield power in selfless ways, we are

in line with God's way of acting and our actions can become even more empowered.

The universe's ability to reveal "great and unsearchable things we do not know" and answer so many of our questions, is evidence of the mind of a God who "formed it and established it" and personally answers us ("Call to me and I will answer you"). When scientific efforts find an answer, we can be reminded of the God who answers us and that every answer is personal. The answer to the question of the meaning of life that scientists (and all human beings) seek lies right behind, before, and above creation's truths. We need to call to God, and God will answer us.

> **The unbreakable nature of the divine covenant with creation assures us that God's promises to humanity are trustworthy—as trustworthy as the universe is stable.**

The unbreakable nature of the divine covenant with creation assures us that God's promises to humanity are trustworthy—as trustworthy as the universe is stable.

Each of these prophecies calls us to live into the connection between our choices and God's choices, between our actions and God's. The more we know God through creation, the more we'll know how to live in Godlike ways. Even as God cites the witness of creation as evidence of God's faithful presence, we can do the same. By knowing God through science—how wide and high and deep and long God's faithfulness in the cosmos is—we can do the right thing, make better moral and ethical decisions, wield our power for the benefit of others, and work through theological challenges.

The fact that God chose creation as a source of revelation should inspire us to steward God's physical Word with reverence. God speaks through a world we're called to care for!

By knowing God through creation, as seen and understood through the lens of the Scriptures, we'll know how to live our lives.

A PERSONAL STORY

Years ago, I was in the middle of a big life transition; I felt anxious and weak and didn't know what God wanted me to do. As I waited, my faith wavered. I prayed for the ability to trust God more.

That trust came while I was out for a walk one day. I had decided to engage in a thought experiment. In my imagination I held two thoughts together—the fact that at that very moment the DNA in my body was repairing itself trillions of times per second and that my body, walking on the face of this planet, in this solar system, within this galaxy, was currently flying along at 1.9 million mph relative to the universe itself.

Knowing that God was providentially holding both of these things—the infinitesimal and infinite—I tried to imagine God sustaining everything in between—the biomechanics of my knees, each tree branch on my path, the earth's hydrological cycle, the global economy, etc.

At first it was hard to keep my balance. But then, for just a few seconds, I sensed God holding everything together. In the power of that moment, I started to pray about my life.

As I prayed, I knew I wasn't asking for things that were out of God's control or that were impossible to accomplish. I was asking for things that were already, in every sense imaginable, held by God. Something about keeping God's faithful actions in creation in mind gave me the faith to trust God's promises to me (as I knew them through the Bible).

YOUR STORY

Knowing God's presence through creation can give you a faith that enables you to see where you need to go and know what you need to say. Even as God's plant-science revelation through branches can shape how you uniquely branch out into the world, God's wisdom through every facet of creation can be your guide.

Listen to God's agrarian word through the prophet Isaiah:

Listen and hear my voice;
    pay attention and hear what I say.
When a farmer plows for planting, does he plow continually?
    Does he keep on breaking up and working the soil?
When he has leveled the surface,
    does he not sow caraway and scatter cumin?
Does he not plant wheat in its place,
    barley in its plot,
    and spelt in its field?
His God instructs him
    and teaches him the right way.

Caraway is not threshed with a sledge,
    nor is the wheel of a cart rolled over cumin;
caraway is beaten out with a rod,
    and cumin with a stick.
Grain must be ground to make bread;
    so one does not go on threshing it forever.
The wheels of a threshing cart may be rolled over it,
    but one does not use horses to grind grain.
All this also comes from the LORD Almighty,
    whose plan is wonderful,
    whose wisdom is magnificent. **ISA. 28:23-29,** emphasis mine

See how the natural properties of caraway and cumin—built into them by God—come together with the farmer's human (scientific) knowledge of how best to handle caraway and cumin? Even as there are ways of operating that God has providentially built into nature, there are ways God has built into human nature and the cultural products and technologies of human nature.

God's cosmic plan is wonderful, and His wisdom is magnificent. Our cultural products are borne out of who we are in relation to the world God made. Engaging God's revelation in the phases of this process—via nature, our image-bearing natures, and the nature of the cultural products we create—will help provide us with necessary checks and balances. If the best iteration of each of these phases is founded on, and in sync with, God's wisdom, then the more we seek to engage God's wisdom in each phase (for example, attending to God's revelation through soil, farmer, and produce), the better the chance all the pieces will fit together.

Listening to God through the soil, we'll know how to treat the soil and by treating the soil in Godlike ways we'll grow what's best for the soil and us. Growing what's best for the soil and us will yield a kind of produce that is just right in terms of God's long-term, eco-sustaining plan. The best way to ensure wise action in accordance with God's plan is to engage God's revelation in each phase.

When you consider how revelation informs behavior, could it be that science needs the church just as much as the church needs science? God can use each to enhance the other by exposing their limitations and affirming the need to engage God's revelation wherever it appears.

John Calvin said, "If we regard the Spirit of God as the sole fountain of truth, we shall neither reject the truth itself, nor despise wherever it shall appear, unless we wish to dishonor the Spirit of God. For by holding the gifts of the Spirit in slight esteem, we contemn

[*show contempt toward*] and reproach the Spirit himself."[6]

If the church holds the gifts of the Spirit—which shine through all that is good and true in science—in slight esteem, we're showing contempt toward and reproaching the Spirit.

Perhaps now is the time for the church to repent and humble itself and listen anew to *all* that God is saying—especially in relation to all that science is unveiling.

LECTIO SCIENTIA

The Chemistry of Creation Care

For most of my life I have been negligently indifferent to the ongoing environmental catastrophe of plastic waste. Like many on our planet, my consumption rate was high and my recycling efforts low. I was a big part of the problem until I preached a sermon on the theology of plastic, chemistry, and catalysis and discovered the amazing science that has enabled plastic (and all the good that has come from it to our world) to even exist.

I interviewed chemist Daryll Harrison about a critical discovery his team at Nova Chemicals made in the late 1990s that led to the creation of a new billion-dollar industry (a catalyst that enabled thinner, cleaner, stiffer, lighter, and stronger plastics). I asked him to unpack the moment when he realized what they had—to tell me what it felt like, how it made him more human. "I've always been intrigued by molecule making," he responded. "You're creating something that's new and not previously known. So I was first excited that we had a scientific result—an amazing scientific discovery. No one anywhere in the world had conceived that this molecule would be capable of doing what it appeared to be capable of doing. Here we had it in our hands."[7]

Hearing Daryll Harrison say these words, Jesus' parable of the pearl of great price came to mind: "God's kingdom is like a jewel merchant on the hunt for exquisite pearls. Finding one that is flawless, he immediately sells everything and buys it" (Matt. 13:45–46 MSG).

For years, Harrison and his team were on the hunt for an exquisite molecule. When they found one with such outstanding capabilities, they were stunned. Knowing what they had, the company they worked for pivoted and invested huge sums into creating a whole new arm of the plastics industry.

In a very real sense Nova Chemicals responded like the biblical jewel merchant in the parable. Because they had scientists and engineers who knew their stuff, Nova Chemicals was able to see this new molecule for what it was. Seeing it for "what it was" inspired them to do whatever it took to "possess" it more fully and see it through to its full potential.

Moments of great discovery are often preceded by a long search for something better, something amazing, something more. For discoveries to be truly appreciated, there must be people who can see the discoveries for what they are. We need jewel merchants and chemists! For the discoveries to be stewarded appropriately, these same experts need to inspire and lead further efforts. There is something about knowing the goodness of what you possess that enables you to steward that goodness in the best possible way.

PRACTICE

Because science enables us to intimately know the goodness of creation, it stands to reason that scientists might know best when it comes to stewarding creation. Yet, if you're like me, you may not be listening to all those scientists (environmental, plant and marine biologists, zoologists, chemists, and physicists) as well as you could.

Consider making it a practice to listen more attentively.

What if you identify the biggest environmental challenge now playing out in the place where you live (e.g., an endangered species, a polluting industry, forest mismanagement, water problems) and invest some time into researching the basic science behind the problem. Don't just let the science identify what's wrong; let it help you better understand what's right. Let the science reveal creation's glory in such a way and to such an extent that it enables you to know and appreciate what the experts know (and what God knows!).

For me, it took a greater appreciation of what one single molecule could do to inspire me to more attentively steward the products made possible by that molecule. How might this play out for you? Perhaps you could write your own personal enviro-parable: "The kingdom of heaven is like a follower of Jesus who started to research the plight of the snowy owl, manatee, or old growth forest . . ."

PRAY

Lord, help us better understand the way You feel about this world You've made. Help us love it like You do. Give us a knowledge that begets a wisdom to steward it in a way that honors You, that honors all You have made.

GOD'S VISION FOR CREATION

"I am making all things new."

REVELATION 21:5 ESV

In the Old Testament book of Ezekiel, the prophet is given a vision of God's future plans—literally in terms of the design of a temple and figuratively in relation to God's ultimate goal for the cosmos.

Amid chapters of prescriptive architectural detail, God says to Ezekiel, "Son of man, describe the temple to the people of Israel, that they may be ashamed of their sins. Let them consider its perfection" (Ezek. 43:10). Great design can have humbling effects. When science reveals God's design for the universe, we should all fall to our knees. What a mind. What power.

Commenting on the book of Genesis, theologian John Walton argues that its first words are meant to teach us that creation is God's "cosmic temple."[1] Where Genesis 1 speaks of God resting on the seventh day, that "rest," says Walton, should be understood as taking up residence. God didn't need a break but wanted a home. This plan was affirmed when God "moved into the neighborhood" through

Christ's incarnation (John 1:14 MSG). At the end of the Bible we read, "Look! God's dwelling place is now among the people, and he will dwell with them. They will be his people, and God himself will be with them and be their God. 'He will wipe every tear from their eyes. There will be no more death' or mourning or crying or pain, for the old order of things has passed away" (Rev. 21:34).

> **Human beings are meant to live in harmony with a creation that will one day be made perfect.**

God's ultimate cosmic plan is for everyone and everything to live in perfect communion with God. Because of this communion, we'll engage creation as we were meant to—as a God-revealing text that must be responsibly stewarded. Human beings are meant to live in harmony with a creation that will one day be made perfect. Jesus says, "I am making all things new" (Rev. 21:5).

A big part of this ongoing renewal process happens through the work of science. Science reveals the nature of God's home—its original design, how to take care of it, and its tremendous long-term potential. From Aristotle's first empirical thoughts to the scientific revolutions of the Middle, Modern, and Post-Modern Ages, science has become a wellspring that has enabled incredible human flourishing. This gift flows from the mind of God in accordance with a perfect plan. When science brings flourishing, it foreshadows a one-day perfect flourishing. Knowing God's endgame can also have a "calling" or "pulling" effect.

After God described the temple's design to the prophet Ezekiel, God pointed to a small trickle of water coming from its threshold. From this hidden spring a cosmic plan flowed. Just outside the temple the water was ankle deep, a third of a mile further it was knee deep, then it was waist deep, and finally impassible—a "river that [no one] could cross" (Ezek. 47:5). God asks Ezekiel, "Do you see this?"

Then he led me back to the bank of the river. When I arrived there, I saw a great number of trees on each side of the river. He said to me, "This water flows toward the eastern region and goes down into the Arabah, where it enters the Dead Sea. When it empties into the sea, the salty water there becomes fresh. Swarms of living creatures will live wherever the river flows. There will be large numbers of fish, because this water flows there and makes the salt water fresh; so where the river flows everything will live. Fishermen will stand along the shore; from En Gedi to En Eglaim there will be places for spreading nets . . . Fruit trees of all kinds will grow on both banks of the river. Their leaves will not wither, nor will their fruit fail. Every month they will bear fruit, because the water from the sanctuary flows to them. Their fruit will serve for food and their leaves for healing." **EZEK. 47:6-12**

God makes saltwater fresh and brings new life to everything. The images of a life-giving river and healing leaves are echoed in Revelation's heavenly vision:

Then the angel showed me the river of the water of life, as clear as crystal, flowing from the throne of God and of the Lamb down the middle of the great street of the city. On each side of the river stood the tree of life, bearing twelve crops of fruit, yielding its fruit every month. And the leaves of the tree are for the healing of the nations. No longer will there be any curse. The throne of God and of the Lamb will be in the city, and his servants will serve him. They will see his face, and his name will be on their foreheads. There will be no more night. They will not need the light of a lamp or the light of the sun, for the Lord God will give them light. **REV. 22:1-5**

One day the rift between science and faith will be restored, and we'll all know God perfectly and forever.

This is what the LORD says: "Heaven is my throne,
and the earth is my footstool.
Where is the house you will build for me?
Where will my resting place be?"

ISAIAH 66:1

The LORD is in his holy temple;
let all the earth be silent before him.

HABAKKUK 2:20

"And the name of the city from that time
on will be: THE LORD IS THERE."

EZEKIEL 48:35

ACKNOWLEDGMENTS

Sir John Templeton believed the nature of the universe revealed something of the Creator. In 1987, he formed a foundation to help bring faith and science together. This book would not exist were it not for his generous vision. Through my involvement with several John Templeton Foundation funded projects—Regent College's *Cosmos, Scientists in Congregations,* Fuller Seminary's *STEAM,* Ambrose Seminary's *Science for Seminaries,* and a Sinai and Synapses fellowship supported by The Issachar Fund—I was able to participate in a deeply illuminating conversation on the intersection of faith and science. Over the past ten years, dozens of scientists—atheist, agnostic, and persons of faith—have helped me research and write numerous science-based sermons, articles, and book chapters. I am deeply indebted to all these people.

I am also thankful to those who helped shape and bring this book together: my son Thomas who helped me learn the language of science, friends who read early rough drafts, editors at every stage, my agent (and former publisher) Don Pape, Drew Dyck for checking out a book based on a Twitter pitch, Moody Publishers for taking on a unique project, and to those who graciously listened to many science-based sermons over the years.

NOTES

Introduction: Engaging God through All Things

1. Guido de Bres, *Belgic Confession* (Grand Rapids: Faith Alive Christian Resources, 2011), Article 2.

2. John Calvin, *Calvin: Institutes of the Christian Religion*, The Library of Christian Classics (Louisville, KY: Presbyterian Publishing Corporation, 1960), I.xiv.1, Kindle.

3. Ibid., I.v.8; 2.vi.1.

4. Johannes Kepler, letter (April 9/10, 1599) to the Bavarian chancellor Herwart von Hohenburg, in Carola Baumgardt, *Johannes Kepler Life and Letters* (London: Gollancz, 1953), 50.

5. Abraham Kuyper, *Wisdom and Wonder* (Grand Rapids: Christian's Library Press, 2011), 39.

6. Herman Bavinck, *The Philosophy of Revelation* (Ancaster, Ontario: Alev Books, 2011), 20.

7. Walter Brueggemann, *The Prophetic Imagination* (Philadelphia: Fortress Press, 1978), 23.

8. Ibid., 44.

9. Richard J. Foster, *Celebration of Discipline: The Path to Spiritual Growth* (New York: HarperCollins, 1998), 3.

10. Ibid., 2.

11. John Calvin, quoted in Belden Lane, *Ravished by Beauty: The Surprising Legacy of Reformed Spirituality* (New York: Oxford University Press, 2011), 74. I'm indebted to Belden Lane for his thoughts on the revelatory nature of creation and for pointing me to helpful material from several writers.

Chapter 1: Radiation Therapy and the Empirical Mind of God

1. John (Jack) Cunningham, *And I Thought I Came from a Cabbage Patch! (A Memoir)*, 2nd ed. (self-published, 2014), 246–47.

2. Faiz M. Khan, *Our Universe: A Scientific and Religious View of Creation* (Lincoln, NE: iUniverse, 2007), x.

3. Ibid., 175.

4. John C. Polkinghorne, "The Creation and Structure of the Physical World," Reformation Christian Ministries, Reformation.edu, https://www.reformation.edu/scripture-science-stott/aarch/pages/06-polkinghorne-creation.htm.

5. Jacob Van Dyk, phone interview, June 2014, Calgary, Alberta.

6. Ibid.

7. Ibid.

8. Greg Bootsma, email interview, June 2014.

9. Van Dyk interview.

10. Ibid.

11. Ibid.

Chapter 2: Supernovae and God's Passion for Matter

1. From the introduction.

2. Mars Rover researcher/astronomer, email interview, October 2013.

3. Allen Dailey, "How Many Supernovae Explode Each Second in the Universe?" *Astronomy*, August 25, 2008, https://astronomy.com/magazine/ask-astro/2008/08/how-many-supernovae-explode-each-second-in-the-universe.

4. Gordon J. Spykman, *Reformational Theology: A New Paradigm for Doing Dogmatics* (Grand Rapids: Eerdmans, 1992), 553.

5. Jürgen Moltmann, quoted in Steven R. Guthrie, *Creator Spirit: The Holy Spirit and the Art of Becoming Human* (Grand Rapids: Baker, 2011), 158.

6. Ibid.

7. Richard Mouw, *He Shines in All That's Fair: Culture and Common Grace* (Grand Rapids: Eerdmans, 2001,) 35–36.

Chapter 3: Engaging God's Providence through Knees and Fossils

1. Johann H. Diemer, *Nature and Miracle* (Toronto: Wedge Publishing Foundation, 1977), 25.

2. John C. Polkinghorne, *Science and the Trinity: The Christian Encounter with Reality* (New Haven, CT: Yale University Press, 2004).

3. Ibid., 5.

4. Ibid.

5. Ibid.

6. Laurie Hiemstra, personal interview, Banff, Alberta, 2017.

7. Ibid.

8. "The Lord's Day 1," *Heidelberg Cathechism* (1563), Christian Reformed Church (website), www.crcna.org/sites/default/files/lords_day_1.pdf.

9. John Calvin, *Calvin: Institutes of the Christian Religion*, The Library of Christian Classics (Louisville, KY: Presbyterian Publishing Corporation, 1960), Q&A 1, Kindle.

10. Ibid., I.xvi.4.

11. Gordon J. Spykman, *Reformational Theology: A New Paradigm for Doing Dogmatics* (Grand Rapids: Eerdmans, 1992), 272.

12. Ibid., 275.

13. Ibid., 276.

14. Emily Chung, "One Hell of an Impression," *CBC News*, February 23, 2018, https://newsinteractives.cbc.ca/longform/human-footprints-greece.

15. Neil Shubin, *Your Inner Fish: A Journey into the 3.5-Billion-Year History of the Human Body* (Toronto: Random House, 2008), 12.

16. John C. Polkinghorne, "The Creation and Structure of the Physical World," Reformation Christian Ministries, Reformation.edu, https://www.reformation.edu/scripture-science-stott/aarch/pages/06-polkinghorne-creation.htm.

17. Abraham Kuyper, *Wisdom and Wonder* (Grand Rapids: Christian's Library, 2011), 39.

18. See Genesis 18 and Exodus 4.

19. "How Fast Are You Moving Right Now?," Business Insider, October 15, 2006, YouTube video, https://www.youtube.com/watch?v=AM lXzHU-GIU.

20. Ibid.

21. John Calvin, quoted in W. David Taylor, *The Theatre of God's Glory: Calvin, Creation and the Liturgical Arts* (Grand Rapids: Eerdmans, 2017), 91.

Chapter 4: Sensing God's Presence via a Giant Squid

1. Richard Ellis, *The Search for the Giant Squid* (London: Lyons Press, 1998).

2. Ibid.

3. Ibid.

4. Ibid.

5. "Squid Evolved in Marine Wars More Than 100 Million Years Ago," New Scientist, March 1, 2017, https://www.newscientist .com/article/2123118-squid-evolved-in-marine-wars-more-than- 100-million-years-ago/#:~:text=Cephalopods%20%E2%80%93% 20the%20tentacled%20creatures%20that,jet%20propulsion%20 and%20polarised%20vision.

6. John Calvin, *Calvin: Institutes of the Christian Religion*, The Library of Christian Classics (Louisville, KY: Presbyterian Publishing Corporation, 1960), I.iii.1, Kindle.

7. Abraham Kuyper, *Wisdom and Wonder* (Grand Rapids: Christian's Library, 2011), 41.

8. John Locke, quoted in John Bolt, ed., *Herman Bavinck: Essays on Religion, Science, and Society* (Grand Rapids: Baker Academic, 2008), 258.

9. Cara Giaimo, "Found: Gravitational Waves!," Atlas Obscura, February 11, 2016, https://www.atlasobscura.com/articles/found- gravitational-waves.

10. John Van Sloten, "Gravitational Waves and the Voice of God," *ThinkChristian*, February 16, 2016, https://web.archive.orgweb/2021 0726222431/https://thinkchristian.net/gravitational-waves-and-the-voice-of-god?utm_campaign=TC_RSS_Cam paign&utm_source=hs _email&utm_medium=email&utm_content=26346429&_hsenc= p2ANqtz--skYVzNvQuOJ6xF0kIZ3_whrBJ-RVuSSbf6f2EcWKp_ k83Is8WWb6fNFF0vF-FOV0aiX4MtcBaLx6bpuphJB-OTKchxA& _hsmi=26346429.

11. Susan Ashbook Harvey, *Scenting Salvation: Ancient Christianity and the Olfactory Imagination* (Los Angeles: University of California, 2006), 6.

12. Ibid., 125.

13. See Matthew 6:26; 15:10; 26:26; and Luke 24:39.

14. St. Augustine, *The Confessions of Saint Augustine*, trans. Rex Warner (New York: Signet, 2001), XIII, 11, 12.

15. Belden C. Lane, *Ravished by Beauty: The Surprising Legacy of Reformed Spirituality* (New York: Oxford University Press, 2011), 92.

16. Ibid., 103.

Chapter 5: Tree Branches, Wound Healing, and an Interdependent God
1. Vern Peters, telephone interview, April 2014.

2. Ibid.

3. Epigenetics researcher, personal interview, Calgary, Alberta, December 2012.

4. Cymbeline T. Culiat, educator and cofounder and chief scientific officer of NellOne Therapeutics, Inc. (Oak Ridge, Tennesee), email interview, April 2011.

5. Vern Peters interview.

6. Ibid.

7. Lewis Thomas, *Lives of a Cell: Notes of a Biology Watcher* (New York: Penguin Group, 1978), 4.

8. Ivan Semeniuk, "How This Year's Gairdner Winners Are Lighting Up the Brain and Deciphering the Marks on Our Genes," *The Globe and Mail,* March 27, 2018, https://www.theglobeandmail.com/canada/article-how-this-years-gairdner-winners-are-lighting-up-the-brain-and/.

9. Thomas, *Lives of a Cell,* 54.

10. George M. Marsden, *Jonathan Edwards: A Life* (New Haven, CT: Yale University Press, 2003), Kindle location 6334.

11. Edward Dommen and James D. Bratt, eds., *John Calvin Rediscovered: The Impact of His Social and Economic Thought* (Louisville, KY: Westminster John Knox Press, 2007), 53.

12. Ibid.

13. John Calvin, *Calvin: Institutes of the Christian Religion,* The Library of Christian Classics (Louisville, KY: Presbyterian Publishing Corporation, 1960), Kindle location 18504.

Chapter 6: Language Acquisition and a Multilingual God

1. Deb Roy, "The Birth of a Word," TED Conferences, March 2011, https://www.ted.com/talks/deb_roy_the_birth_of_a_word?language=en.

2. St. Augustine, *The First Catechetical Instruction (De Catechizandis Rudibus),* trans. Joseph P. Christopher (Westminster, MD: The Newman Press, 1962), 37.

3. Steven Weinberg, *The First Three Minutes* (New York: Basic Books, 1988), 14.

4. John C. Polkinghorne, *Science and the Trinity: The Christian Encounter with Reality* (New Haven, CT: Yale University Press, 2004), 63.

5. C. S. Lewis, *The Weight of Glory: And Other Addresses* (New York: HarperOne, 2001), 30–31.

6. John Calvin, *Calvin: Institutes of the Christian Religion,* The Library of Christian Classics (Louisville, KY: Presbyterian Publishing Corporation, 1960), I.iii.1, Kindle.

7. Marcelo Gleiser, in Krista Tibbet, "Marilynne Robinson and Marcelo Gleiser: The Mystery We Are," *On Being* (podcast), January 8, 2012, https://onbeing.org/programs/marilynne-robinson-marcelo-gleiser-the-mystery-we-are/.

8. Alvin Plantinga, *Warranted Christian Belief* (New York: Oxford University Press, 2000), 175.

9. Michael Polanyi was a scientist and philosopher who first used the label *tacit knowledge*, meaning knowledge we acquire through experience but is difficult to express in words, "knowing more than we can tell." See Anita Kothari et al., "The Use of Tacit and Explicit Knowledge in Public Health," Implementation Science, March 20, 2012, https://implementationscience.biomedcentral.com/articles/10.1186/1748-5908-7-20.

10. Lesslie Newbigin, *Proper Confidence: Faith, Doubt, and Certainty in Christian Discipleship* (Grand Rapids: Eerdmans, 1995), 90.

11. Thomas Soifer, quoted in Douglas Martin, "Gerry Neugebauer, Pioneer in Space Studies, Dies at 82," *New York Times*, October 2, 2014, https://www.nytimes.com/2014/10/03/us/gerry-neugebauer-pioneer-in-space-studies-dies-at-82.html#:~:text=He%20was%2082.,Dr.

12. L. Alonso Schökel, *Manual of Hebrew Poetics* (Rome: Gregorian University Press, 1987), 104.

13. Newbigin, *Proper Confidence*, 42.

14. Ibid, 58.

15. Ibid, 59.

16. Martin Buber, quoted in Newbigin, *Proper Confidence*, 60.

17. Newbigin, *Proper Confidence*, 37.

18. Richard A. Muller, "Crede, ut intelligas," "Credo, ut intelligam," in *Dictionary of Latin and Greek Theological Terms* (Grand Rapids: Baker, 1985).

19. Jan Karon, *A Continual Feast* (New York: Viking, 2006), 6.

20. Newbigin, *Proper Confidence*, 76.

21. Donald N. Petcher, "What Does It Mean to Be Kuyperian?," *The Kuyperian*, April 1996, http://kuyperian.blogspot.com/2004/10/what-does-it-mean-to-be-kuyperian.html.

22. Polkinghorne, *Science and the Trinity*, 90.

23. Ibid.

24. Ibid., 92.

25. Ibid.

26. The Nicene Creed, https://www.crcna.org/welcome/beliefs/creeds/nicene-creed.

27. "How Fast Are You Moving Right Now?," Business Insider, October 15, 2006, YouTube video, https://www.youtube.com/watch?v=AMlXzHU-GIU.

28. Nicholas Chevalier et al., "Myelination Is Associated with Processing Speed in Early Childhood: Preliminary Insights," National Library of Medicine, October 6, 2015, https://pubmed.ncbi.nlm.nih.gov/26440654/.

Chapter 7: God's Beauty in DNA Repair Mechanisms

1. Thomas Dubay, *The Evidential Power of Beauty: Science and Theology Meet* (San Francisco: Ignatius Press, 2006), 56.

2. Dustin Pearson, personal interview, Calgary, Alberta, 2017.

3. Rose Eveleth, "There are 37.2 Trillion Cells in Your Body," *Smithsonian Magazine*, October 24, 2013, https://www.smithsonianmag.com/smart-news/there-are-372-trillion-cells-in-your-body-4941473/.

4. Stephen P. Jackson and Jiri Bartek, "The DNA-Damage Response in Human Biology and Disease," *Nature*, October 22, 2009, https://www.nature.com/articles/nature08467.

5. Pearson interview.

6. Douglas Copeland, *Hey Nostradamus!* (Toronto: Random House, 2004), 233.

7. John Bolt, ed., *Herman Bavinck: Essays on Religion, Science, and Society* (Grand Rapids: Baker Academic, 2008), 247.

8. Ibid.

9. Ibid., 256.

10. See, for example, Psalms 19, 29, and 104. Allen C. Myers, "Glory," in *The Eerdmans Bible Dictionary* (Grand Rapids: Eerdmans, 1987), 420.

11. Allen C. Myers, "Glory," in *The Eerdmans Bible Dictionary* (Grand Rapids: Eerdmans, 1987), 420.

12. John Calvin, *Commentary on the Book of the Prophet Isaiah*, vol. 4 (Edinburgh: Calvin Translation Society, 1853), 194.

13. John Calvin, *Commentaries of the First Book of Moses Called Genesis*, vol. 4 (Woodstock, Ontario: Devoted Publishing, 2018), 20.

14. Philip Sheldrake, "Calvinist Spirituality" in *The New SCM Dictionary of Christian Spirituality* (London: SCM, 2005).

15. Pearson interview.

16. Ibid.

17. St. Irenaeus of Lyons, *The Third Book of St. Irenaeus Against Heresies*, ed. Henry Deane (Oxford: Clarendon Press, 1874), 4.34.5–7.

18. Pearson interview.

19. Bolt, *Herman Bavinck*, 259.

20. Thomas Dubay, *The Evidential Power of Beauty: Science and Theology Meet* (San Francisco: Ignatius, 2006), 16–17.

21. Bolt, *Herman Bavinck*, 256.

22. Dubay, *The Evidential Power of Beauty*, 20.

23. Richard J. Mouw, *Abraham Kuyper: A Short and Personal Introduction* (Grand Rapids: Eerdmans, 2011), 92.

24. St. Irenaeus of Lyons, "Man Fully Alive," Humanum Quarterly, issue 1, 2019, quoting from *Against Heresies*, book IV, chapter 10, no. 6–7, https://humanumreview.com/articles/man-fully-alive.

25. Dubay, *The Evidential Power of Beauty*, 78.

26. Ibid., 79.

27. Ibid., 99.

28. St. Augustine, *The Confessions of Saint Augustine*, trans. Rex Warner (New York: Signet, 2001), 235.

Chapter 8: Naming Creation via Neuroscience

1. A young neuroscientist, personal interview, Calgary, Alberta, May 2013.

2. Ibid.

3. Hebrews 11:13 says, "All these people were still living by faith when they died. They did not receive the things promised; they only saw them and welcomed them from a distance, admitting that they were foreigners and strangers on earth."

4. Anita Li, "Scientists Determine Earth Has 8.7 Million Species," *Globe and Mail*, August 23, 2011, https://www.theglobeandmail. com/technology/science/scientists-determine-earth-has-87-million-species/article591529/.

5. Allen C. Myers, "Name," in *The Eerdmans Bible Dictionary* (Grand Rapids: Eerdmans, 1987), 747.

6. Vilayanur Ramachandran, "The Neurons That Shaped Civilization," TED Conference, November 2009, https://www.ted.com/talks/ vilayanur_ramachandran_the_neurons_that_shaped_civilization? language=en.

7. Ibid.

8. Laser Interferometer Gravitational-Wave Observatory.

9. Ramachandran, "The Neurons That Shaped Civilization."

10. Neuroscientist interview.

11. Murray Gell-Mann, "Beauty, Truth and . . . Physics?," TED Conference, March 2007, https://www.ted.com/talks/murray_ gell_mann_beauty_truth_and_physics?language=en.

12. Catherine La Cugna, quoted in Belden C. Lane, *Ravished by Beauty: The Surprising Legacy of Reformed Spirituality* (New York: Oxford University Press, 2011), 67.

13. Covenant Protestant Reformed Church, "Christ Speaking Through Preaching," https://cprc.co.uk/quotes/christspeakingpreaching/.

14. Lane, *Ravished by Beauty*, 91.

Chapter 9: God's Hydrological Heart in a River

1. Parts of this chapter were adapted from John Van Sloten, "God Was the First Scientist," *Calgary Herald*, September 14, 2019, https://calgaryherald.com/opinion/columnists/god-was-the-first-scientist; John Van Sloten, "God's Witness in the Cosmos," Christian Courier, October 22, 2018, https://www.christiancourier.ca/gods-witness-in-the-cosmos/.

2. Dr. Masaki Hayashi, personal interview, University of Calgary, April 2012.

3. Mary Midgley, quoted by Alister E. McGrath, "Science and Faith: Conflicting or Enriching?," Regent InterFace, September 18, 2018, video, 18:15, https://www.regentinterface.com/topics/science-and-faith/.

4. Ibid., 24:02.

5. Gordon J. Spykman, *Reformational Theology: A New Paradigm for Doing Dogmatics* (Grand Rapids: Eerdmans, 1992), 270.

6. John Calvin, *Calvin: Institutes of the Christian Religion*, The Library of Christian Classics (Louisville, KY: Presbyterian Publishing Corporation, 1960), 2.ii.15, Kindle.

7. Daryll Harrison, Zoom interview, Calgary, November 2020.

Epilogue: God's Vision for Creation

1. David Buller, "Creation Is the Temple Where God Rests," BioLogos, March 6, 2015, https://biologos.org/articles/series/reflections-on-the-lost-world-of-genesis-1-by-john-walton/creation-is-the-temple-where-god-rests.

RETURN TO CREATION.
ENCOUNTER THE CREATOR.

MOODY Publishers®

From the Word to Life®

Turning of Days beckons you to a world of tree frogs and peach blossoms, mountain springs and dark winter nights—all in search of nature's God, all in harmony with Scripture. Join Hannah Anderson, author of *Humble Roots*, as she journeys through the four seasons in this collection of devotional essays and illustrations. Take a look, and see His glory everywhere.

978-0-8024-1856-2 | also available as an eBook and audiobook

COULD BRAIN SCIENCE BE THE KEY TO SPIRITUAL FORMATION?

OUR CONSTANT DANGER IS THAT WE HAVE A VIEW OF GOD THAT IS TOO SMALL.

MOODY Publishers®

From the Word to Life®

With pastoral warmth and heart, Griffiths shows us God in all His beauty and goodness. Readers will gain knowledge of God's attributes. Through this knowledge, trust, hope, and joy emerge. Confidence and faith grow stronger.

978-0-8024-7396-7 | also available as an eBook and audiobook